The Area Specialist Bibliographer: An Inquiry into His Role

by

ROBERT D. STUEART

The Scarecrow Press, Inc.
Metuchen, N.J.   1972

Copyright 1972 by Robert D. Stueart

Library of Congress Cataloging in Publication Data

Stueart, Robert D
    The area specialist bibliographer.

    Bibliography: p.
    1. Area specialist bibliographers--U. S.
2. College librarians--U. S.   I. Title.
Z6201.A2S85   010   72-1300
ISBN 0-8108-0487-5

For Marlies

PREFACE

There are many professional-specialist groups now
working in libraries. Among them is the area specialist
bibliographer who is chosen as the subject of this inquiry because he now holds a key position. in the library. His thinking and behavior are influences on the attitudes, values and
behavior of faculty, library administrators and fellow employees. There is general agreement on the need for such
a person but there is no agreement on what his role should
actually be.

It is the intent of this volume to develop a model designed to eliminate present difficulties and ambiguities and
to improve administrative procedures for future development
of area programs. This will be accomplished by giving
some indication of the climate of opinion toward area specialist bibliographers and by isolating factors which influence
these opinions. These attitudes will be presented by the
perceptions of area bibliographers toward their role and the
expectations of faculty and library administrators toward that
role. The bibliographer's academic, professional, and educational experience will be examined in this framework.

Many individuals--the faculty members, library administrators, and especially the area specialist bibliographers
--who contributed significantly to this study must remain
anonymous. Others deserve explicit acknowledgment: Dr.
Jay E. Daily for his friendship, encouragement, and guid-
ance in the development of this study; other committee

v

members for my dissertation from which this present volume evolved--Drs. Philip Immroth, Martha Manheimer, Donald Shirey, Harold Lancour and Frank Sessa; Jim Williams, whose assistance was invaluable; my aunt, Helen Roberts, who so graciously agreed to type the final manuscript; the panel of experts who impelled the research through their suggestions; and, finally, my wife Marlies who shared both the joy and anguish of this effort. To all of these I owe a debt of gratitude.

CONTENTS

LIST OF TABLES

LIST OF ILLUSTRATIONS

INTRODUCTION

Somewhere among the accumulation of his memora-
bilia, there is a certificate stating that the undersigned is
a graduate of the Army Specialized Training Program at
Grinnell College. It is dated 1944 and represents six
months of intense study of Spain and Spanish. Just why the
Army chose to take a private first class and give him this
education remained a mystery until now. The recipient was
always grateful though, and it is quite appropriate that he
introduce the study that follows.

It is almost an accident that this is a doctoral dissertation, the result of the most international of all programs of studies. It would have to be written as a treatise
if no completion of requirements had been involved. Un-
like some dissertations that help the reader learn more
and more about less and less, this work strikes at a common problem in academic institutions and aims at something more than an exercise in research methodology. It
is meant to be useful to librarians, department chairmen,
and other administrators in Academe. The question that
underlies the study is this: just how scholarly is librarianship, how much claim to advancement for reasons other
than administrative responsibility do librarians have?
Equally, it provides a means of improving the scholarly
contribution of the only generalists whose field is recorded
knowledge. As the present avalanche of information bears
down upon us, hopefully to increase in volume and value,

specialists are required who combine talents, experience, and abilities heretofore unknown, or at least not clearly isolated. If any professional group has troubles of identity, it is that remarkable general specialist (or special generalist), the bibliographer in language and area studies. As the author states, his role has been so ill-defined that the language and area bibliographer thinks of himself as a generalist only because he has so many widely different duties.

A good dissertation does not provide a solution, it clarifies a problem and reveals how it is linked to other problems. Usually a clearly stated administrative problem will provide for as many solutions as there are places where attention is focussed on the needs, peculiarities, and expectations of the particular institution. The university libraries of the United States represent the greatest gathering of information in the history of mankind, far exceeding anything that can be found abroad or that has existed in the past. To maintain the leadership, improve the service, and assist in the advance of knowledge, the faculty in the classroom rely on the assistance of an information specialist. It is nothing less than amazing that no clear definition of roles and of the interaction of needs and services has been made to date. The lacuna is filled here in a valid and comprehensive fashion.

However, something more than language and area studies is involved. By simple analogy, much of the investigative procedure relates to any person in a library performing any kind of service. Some meeting of minds on what is expected and what is possible is the forerunner of an effective and profitable program. Profitable, as is always the case in libraries, not in terms of monetary return but in the far more significant area of intangible values.

The story goes that a university faculty, during World War II, was beginning to organize itself as a policy forming body, seeking to alleviate the administrative pressure the faculty found unbearable, especially in view of low status and poor pay. A solemn vote was taken on whether to include librarians among the faculty members, and at last "the lunatic fringe," as they were called, were admitted. The description may be less denigrating in the numerous places where the same drama has been enacted with different characters and under different circumstances, but librarians have generally been second-class citizens in the ranks of those whose task is to provide education. They gain full status only when they deserve it by exhibiting what scholars admire most, scholarship. It takes some effort to convince university faculty members that librarians can do much to make schooling and education actually synonymous rather than practically independent. The ultimate benefit goes where it belongs, to the student. The undersigned only regrets that his efforts on behalf of the librarians at his university could not have had the advantage of this study as a preliminary. In acting as the lawyer who got legislation through the Senate Council and the Senate, the undersigned had to rely on fancy footwork, eloquent appeals, and everything but what he needed most, sound scholarship.

An advisor and a student make an academic multitude. The student instructs the advisor and the advisor becomes a better student, hence a better teacher. In this sharing of enterprise (though not of effort--any author of a dissertation far exceeds in his effort what any advisor can do) the happiest result, aside from the advancement of knowledge,

xv

is the explanation the advisor gets of parts of his experience, his role, and his expectations. At last, so many years later, the undersigned sees why he is an alumnus of the Army Specialized Training Program in Spanish at Grinnell College. It was all meant to prepare him for his happy and rewarding part in bringing this study to light.

Jay E. Daily

Pittsburgh, Pa.
20 July 1971

Chapter I

AREA STUDY PROGRAMS IN UNIVERSITIES

> Today, universities face the greatest challenge in
> their histories . . . The need to maintain a faculty
> that, combined with the students, makes up an
> outstanding community of scholars will post a con-
> tinuing and growing challenge to universities in
> light of . . . increases in number of new academic
> programs, particularly in interdisciplinary areas,
> such as foreign area studies . . . [1]

Universities have been confronted with problems of
expanding curricula and research in various fields of knowledge. These changes immediately affect the resources and
services of the library. Structure and growth of populations
served, changing nature of curricula, newer teaching methods,
the emergence of the graduate school, greater emphasis on
research, all demand adequate library collections and services for these collections, and pose serious administrative
problems in academic libraries. To this list must now be
added the "area studies" programs that have emerged since
World War II but received their greatest impetus after the
launching of Sputnik in 1958. These non-Western studies
comprise all the areas of the world except Western Europe
and North America. Areas involved are South, Southeast,
and East Asia; the Near East; Africa; Latin America; and
the Soviet Union and East Europe; areas representing five-
sixths of the population of the world.

Most universities now include courses in non-Western

studies.   Colleges have also created area language and literature studies for the undergraduate.   Through the years,
focus on the contemporary period has posed different problems for different areas.

> Compare, on one hand, China with thousands of
> years of written literature and a history of unity
> and continuity and, on the other hand, sub-Saharan
> Africa without such written records, without his-
> torical or linguistic unity, but with a recent co-
> lonial experience under European administration,
> education, and languages.   Or contrast Near East-
> ern studies, with relative linguistic and religious
> diversity but a strongly centralized state.   Or
> contrast the linguistic diversity, colonial experi-
> ence, large population, and political unity of India
> with the relative linguistic simplicity, but political
> fragmentation of Latin America. [2]

The impact on libraries in academic institutions has
been immense.   Because of increased demands for materials
from areas previously not covered in acquisitions programs,
the lack of systematic bibliographical coverage in these
areas, an almost non-existent book trade, and the exotic
languages of these publications, additional burdens have been
imposed on the library staffs, both in acquisition and processing and in selecting and servicing the materials.   A
brief history derived from articles and monographs dealing
in general with area studies and revealing the importance of
library resources in the development of area study programs
is worth reviewing here as elaboration of this statement.

> Non-Western studies have long had scholarly
> devotees.   Sinologists, Indologists (or Sanskritists),
> and Arabists have always played a role in the aca-
> demic world.   They have traditionally been the
> scholars who study, partly out of interest and
> partly for lack of colleagues, the totality of those
> cultures and civilizations.   Stemming, however,
> largely from the fields of classical language and

> literature, archaeology, and the history of art or
> religion, they did not typically apply the insights
> of social science or manifest the interest in con-
> temporary developments which have come to be
> associated with area studies. And they were
> usually not concerned with the modern languages
> spoken in their areas. [3]

Some of these earlier classical programs date back
to the missionary orientation of early denominational colleges.
Some courses were offered in "exotic" languages and anthro-
pologists were concerned with the area concept, but mostly
as it related to primitive groups.   By the 1930's several
distinguished programs had been developed, such as those at
the University of Pennsylvania (South Asia), Yale (Southeast
Asia), and Princeton (Middle East), the China Program at
Cornell and the Latin American program at Texas.   These
were the first efforts at co-ordinating research and teaching
on specific areas.   For the most part, however, there
appears to have been an almost complete lack of language
facilities, and even the culture, history, politics, and
geography of these non-Western nations were not well known
until the Second World War.

The complex military and political situations brought
on by the war awakened this country to the need for knowledge, gained only through studying scholarly resources, about
other countries.   One of the consequences of the Japanese attack
on Pearl Harbor was a military demand for trained Asian
linguists and translators.   Later, the East European
languages received much attention.   Crash language programs were established in several places.   The Army established Specialized Training Programs in 55 universities
and Civil Affairs Training Programs at 10 universities. [4]
"This increasing involvement of the United States with the

world beyond its borders forced the academic community to re-evaluate American education's traditional emphasis on Western studies. "[5]

During this period, "so sparse were our scholarly resources [in area studies] that those who knew anything about the major non-Western areas had to be grouped together in teams in order to cooperate with and supplement each other, thus laying the foundation for the area centers and research programs that universities set up after the war, "[6] after the army had abandoned most of its efforts.

As late as 1947 Wendell C. Bennett pointed out the "woeful lack of area experts, however defined..."[7] The critical need at that time was for competent area specialists, adequate library resources, and well supported programs. [8]

Major universities began to establish some sort of area program in the early 1950's. Centers, institutes, and interdepartmental committees were initiated all over the country. To help establish standards and provide guidelines to institutions seeking support or to the foundations considering requests, the Social Science Research Council set down criteria it deemed necessary for an effective area program:

1. Official university recognition and support of the program;

2. Adequate library resources for teaching and research in the area;

3. Competent instruction in the principle languages of the area;

4. Offerings in at least five pertinent subjects in addition to language instructions;

5. Some specific mechanisms for integrating the area studies;

6. An area research program; and

7. Emphasis on the contemporary aspects of
the area. [9]

The area programs as they emerged showed various
patterns of organization. In general, the pattern established
was that courses were offered by individual departments but
were coordinated through an interdepartmental committee
which was responsible for policies concerning the overall
program. From this core grew the center or institute concept which deals with the different non-Western areas of
the world.

The basic concept of an area study is that the population of a definable geographic area, interacting in their
social and political environment, offer an opportunity for
concentrated study. The area center, then, blends the sub-
stance of several university departments into coherent sets
of courses focusing on that specific region of the world.
Traditionally history, anthropology, geography, languages
and literature, economics, political science, and sociology
have been included in area studies programs. Law, international education, fine arts, religion, philosophy, and folk-
lore are also included in some cases.

One of the problems area studies encountered in the
beginning was the skepticism they met in academic communities. The curricula overlapped traditional fields and
were, no doubt, motivated by international policy. But
these area institutes, centers, or programs, as they are
variously called, did not so much displace traditional departments as they overlapped both in faculty and in course
offerings. Area programs have always been in the main-
stream of the continuing effort to adjust and correct the

rigid organizational pattern of universities.   This is not to
say that area studies were the first and only interdisciplinary
studies which have developed in universities.

Good examples
also exist in the sciences: biophysics, astrophysics, bio-
medicine, sanitary engineering, and radio astronomy, most
of which have become by now separate disciplines themselves.

There have been several surveys to determine the
number of area programs in operation at a specific time
(see Bibliography: Hall, 1946; Bennett, 1951; Department
of State, 1954, 1956, 1959; Area Study Programs in American U. , 1962, 1964).   McNiff reports that

> In 1946, there were but thirteen operating area
> programs; four for East Asia, six for Latin
> America, and three for Russia and Eastern
> Europe.   There were no programs for Africa,
> South and Southeast Asia or the Near East.   In
> 1962 there were one hundred thirty-five programs
> in sixty-two universities, including thirteen pro-
> grams for Africa, twelve for South and Southeast
> Asia, and seventeen for the Near East. [10]

Societies early played a large role in the development
of area studies.   In 1926 a Committee on Indic and Iranian
Studies, under the auspices of the American Oriental Society,
was founded.   It became a committee of the American
Council of Learned Societies in 1930.   Aided by the Carnegie Corporation, the Committee was influential in establishing what is now the South Asia Section of the Library of
Congress.   In 1946 the Committee on World Area Research
of the Social Science Research Council replaced the Ethnographic Board which had been established in the late 1920's
at the Smithsonian Institution by the National Research
Council, the Social Science Research Council, and the American Council of Learned Societies.   Several other committees,
supported by foundations, have played a large part in the

development of area studies. For example, "The Joint Committee on Slavic Studies . . . joined with the Association of Research Libraries in 1959 in the establishment of a co-ordinating Committee for Slavic and East European Library Resources, which in turn has made critical surveys of library and bibliographical needs and sponsored projects to meet these needs. "[11] The Ruggles-Mostecky[12] study is a good example of the extensive area research that is being carried on by this organization.

The Rockefeller Foundation began to encourage non-Western studies, as early as 1933, by supporting Near East, Slavic, Latin American, and East Asian language and area programs in institutions of higher education. It was followed by the Carnegie Corporation in 1947, which supported studies on the Near East and Latin America also, as well as research on Japan, India, and Southeast Asia. However, it was not until the Ford Foundation entered the picture in 1951 that large foundation grants were allocated to ". . . improve American competence to deal with international problems by narrowing the gap between the needs for and the supply of trained personnel and knowledge. "[13]

The greatest federal funding came in 1958 after the Soviet Union launched Sputnik. The federal aid came in the form of the National Defense Education Act (NDEA), which was mainly concerned with the teaching of science and non-Western languages. NDEA centers were established as a first move by the federal government to accept its responsibilities in the international education area. Nearly $100 million of federal funds were spent in the first ten years of the life of NDEA and enrollment in NDEA area programs grew from 18,000 in 1958 to 71,000 in 1965. [14] A second important act, the International Education Act of 1966, aimed at supplementing NDEA, has unfortunately not materialized.

These three participants then--government, universities and foundations--have complemented each other in the
development of area studies in universities.

In the beginning of area studies, as has been stated
before, three primary needs emerged: (1) the need for competent area specialists, (2) adequate library resources, and
(3) well supported programs. Indications now are that the
need for competent area specialists has been fulfilled. Federal funds, foundation support and university commitments
have also supplied the last of these primary needs: well
supported programs. The provision of adequate library resources, both in materials and personnel, seems to be the
weakest link in the chain. Government support for area resources in academic libraries has come from the 1958 Din-
gell amendment to the Agricultural Trade Development and
Assistance Act of 1954, known as PL 480, providing materials from India, Pakistan, Nepal, Ceylon, Indonesia, United
Arab Republic, Israel and Yugoslavia; and more recently
from the National Program for Acquisitions and Cataloging,
administered through the Library of Congress under the
Higher Education Act of 1965, which has facilitated regional
acquisitions centers in Nairobi, Rio de Janeiro and Djakarta
as well as offices in six other non-Western countries: Bul-
garia, Czechoslovakia, Japan, South Africa, USSR, and Yugoslavia.

The base of competence on non-Western areas has
continued to expand and universities are constantly re-evalu-
ating their activities along those lines of expansion. Despite
this fact, ". . . there are those who suspect that percentage-
wise there may even be less measurable concern with the
non-Western world in our academia now than there was twen-

ty-five years ago. This could, of course, be interpreted as meaning only that our facilities and materials have expanded faster than our personnel available to service them. "[15] A close analysis of this attitude needs to be made, particularly in light of the fact that two-thirds of the books now being acquired by Harvard, the largest university library in this country, are in foreign languages. [16]

It is unnecessary here, and probably impossible, to trace the development of library resources of non-Western materials in the major academic libraries. It is also un- necessary to describe these collections. Suffice it to say that they do exist in varying degrees of comprehensiveness in most of the major academic libraries. Several surveys have addressed themselves to this point in some detail.

The University of Chicago Graduate Library School, in its 1964 annual conference, concentrated on "Area Studies and the Library. "[17] In the introduction to that conference it was stated,

> The introduction of many and varied teaching and research programs focusing on certain geographi- cal or cultural areas is one of the most significant developments in American higher education during the postwar period. These programs aim to pre- pare specialists for deep and comprehensive under- standing of the languages and culture of . . . [the] area . . . which have hitherto been relatively neg- lected in American scholarship. [18]

This conference provided an excellent introduction to the subject of area studies and the important role area bib- liographers should play in developing the library collections.

Several different types of area programs have been created in universities. As a matter of fact, one hundred and forty advanced programs exist in 46 Association of Re- search Library member institutions in this country (see Ap-

Figure 1.   Distribution of Programs
Served by Area Bibliographers
(One hundred and nine programs = 100%)

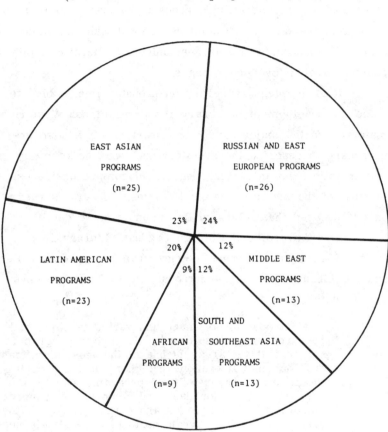

Figure 2.   Geographical Distribution of
Area Specialist Bibliographers

(Dots indicate location of ARL institutions with area programs)

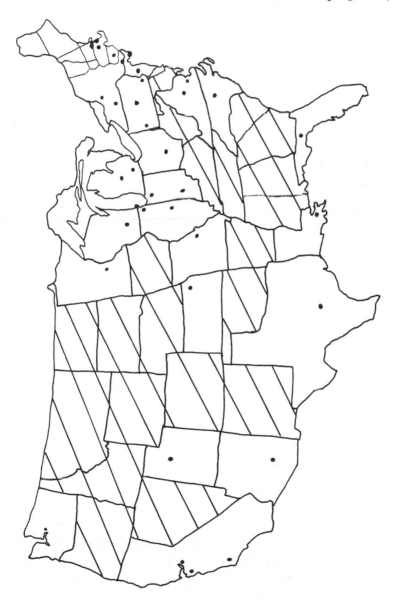

pendix 1). Of those, only 109 were served by area specialist bibliographers at the outset of this study in 1970. The
distribution, by area, is presented in Figure 1. Program
descriptions vary from one university to another. Therefore, for descriptive purposes, arbitrary lines have been
drawn for dividing the programs into the six parts shown.
The greatest difficulty was with the Asian programs. The
following types of programs have been gathered together under the title, East Asian Programs: Oriental, Far Eastern,
Asian, Japanese, Chinese, and East Asian. Russian and
East European Programs include those variously titled:
Slavic, Russian, East Central European, Soviet, and Com-
munist. Middle Eastern Programs are sometimes titled:
Near East and North African, Near Eastern or Islamic. African, Latin American, and South and Southeast Asian Programs are relatively easy to identify in this breakdown.

Most of the area programs are located in universities
which are situated in the Midwest or Northeastern sections
of the United States (see Figure 2).

Notes

1. Association of Research Libraries, Minutes of the Sev-
    enty-fourth Meeting, June 21, 1969, Atlantic City,
    New Jersey (Washington: Association of Research Li-
    braries, 1969), pp. 5-6.

2. Chauncy D. Harris, "Area Studies and Library Re-
    sources," Library Quarterly, XXXV, No. 4 (October,
    1965), 212.

3. U. S. Department of Health, Education, and Welfare,
    Office of Education, NDEA Language and Area Cen-
    ters; A Report of the First Five Years, by Donald N.
    Bigelow and Lyman H. Legters (Washington, D. C. :
    Government Printing Office, 1964), pp. 5-6.

4. Maxwell Flapan, "The World We Have to Know," Amer-
    ican Education, I, No. 8 (October, 1965), 31.

5. U. S. Department of Health, Education and Welfare. Of-
    fice of Education, Language and Area Centers: Title
    VI, National Defense Education Act, 1958-1968 (Wash-
    ington, D. C. : Government Printing Office, 1968),
    p. 1.

6. George E. Taylor, "The Leadership of the Universities,"
    in The Non-Western World in Higher Education, ed.
    by Donald N. Bigelow and Lyman Legters (Philadelph-
    ia: American Academy of Political and Social Sci-
    ences, 1964), p. 3.

7. Robert B. Hall, Area Studies: With Special Reference
    to their Implications for Research in the Social Sci-
    ences, Social Sciences Research Council Pamphlet,
    No. 3 (New York: Social Science Research Council,
    1947), p. iii.

8. Philip J. McNiff, "Foreign Area Studies and their Effect
    on Library Development," College and Research Li-
    braries, XXIV, No. 4 (July, 1963), 292.

9. Wendell C. Bennett, Area Studies in American Univer-
    sities (New York: Social Science Research Council,
    1951), p. 46.

10. McNiff, op. cit. , 293.

11. Harris, op. cit. , 207-208.

12. Melville J. Ruggles and Vaclav Mostecky, Russian and
    East European Publications in Libraries in the United
    States (New York: Columbia University Press, 1960).

13. George M. Beckman, "The Role of the Foundations," in
    The Non-Western World in Higher Education, ed. by
    Donald N. Bigelow and Lyman Legters (Philadelphia:
    American Academy of Political and Social Sciences,
    1964), p. 15.

14. U. S. , Department of Health, Education, and Welfare.
    Office of Education, Language and Area Centers,
    op. cit. , p. 1.

15. Mortimer Graves, The Library of Congress PL-480
    Foreign Acquisitions Program: User's View (New
    York: American Council of Learned Societies, Sep-
    tember, 1969), p. 3.

16. Stephen A. Freeman, "International Study at Home and
    Abroad," in The Non-Western World in Higher Educa-
    tion, ed. by Donald N. Bigelow and Lyman Legters
    (Philadelphia: American Academy of Political and
    Social Sciences, 1964), p. 141.

17. University of Chicago. Graduate Library School, "Pro-
    ceedings of the 13th Annual Conference, May 20-22,
    1965," Library Quarterly, XXXV, No. 4 (October,
    1965).

18. Tsuen-Hsuin Tsien and Howard W. Winger, "Introduc-
    tion," Library Quarterly, XXXV, No. 4 (October,
    1965), 203.

Chapter II

RESEARCH ON THE ROLE OF THE LIBRARIAN

Background Literature

To set the stage properly for a close analysis of the area specialist bibliographer's role in the university, one must first review other studies which have been done on librarians and librarianship.

Very little is known about special personnel resources, among them area specialist bibliographers, and the unique role they probably play in collection development. Maurice Tauber, among others, has suggested a need for a ". . . study of relationships of acquisitions unit[s] to other library units, particularly in connection with foreign acquisitions."[1] It has been said that more is known about how librarians differ from others than about how they differ from each other. There have been no studies, in librarianship, in which the role expectations have been measured and, correspondingly, role performance observed.

The role of the librarian is sociologically a highly viable one, a role which naturally must be in harmony with the library's role, currently in a state of change and confusion. Certain characteristics of a librarian probably indicate his functions in this social structure, define the behavior expected of him, and serve as a guide to his selection. Choosing employees who can relate, effectively, to the clientele, as well as perform adequately, is an important element in library personnel administration. Being aware of

31

this delicate balance, the National Advisory Commission on
Libraries emphasized the need to ". . . provide adequate
trained personnel for the varied and changing demands of
librarianship. "[2]   There is a growing realization, by administrators, that successful management depends upon getting effective results from people.   This approach to the human
aspects of management, i. e. , selection and development of
personnel, has resulted in a growing body of administrative
theory.

    Administrators have been criticized as being more
concerned with putting a man on the job tomorrow than with
answering the more fundamental question of what person, for
what purpose, and with what training, will be needed to foster
and encourage and support the further development of the
field.

    In research studies which have been made on man-
power, in areas of recruitment, education, training, and
utilization, it was found that a limited set of substantial sociological contributions have been made dealing with description and appraisal of professionals in libraries.   A glance at
the library literature on human relations reveals a deluge of
articles decrying or praising the individual library's position
on status, salary, and other "how we done it good" articles.
However, there seem to be relatively few empirical studies
which have tended to estimate, project, or evaluate the nature of the problem.   Even those descriptions of major efforts are, usually, on such a narrow scale that generaliza-
tion is quite risky.   This lack of information, defeating to
confident planning for the future and, indeed, demoralizing
to the profession as a whole, has been recognized by several
agencies: 1) the American Library Association's Ad Hoc
Committee on Manpower Problems, which has recommended

that a series of studies be developed in all types of libraries
to analyze the work done in each library in order to encourage experimentation, demonstration and observation of
the proper use of manpower in libraries; 2) the Association
of Research Libraries' Committee on Training for Research
Librarianship, which is co-ordinating a series of studies to:

> a) determine the kinds of research library services
> to be needed between now and 1980; b) identify the
> level and types of personnel needed to render such
> services; c) describe educational programs neces-
> sary for the preparation of these personnel; d) pro-
> pose a route of change from the training programs
> now available to those anticipated; e) quantify an-
> ticipated personnel needs; f) identify prospective
> new sources of personnel; g) develop programs for
> effective utilization of manpower;[3]

3) a service study going on at the University of Texas Graduate School of Library Science, which will attempt to explore
basic questions about the education of prospective library
personnel in all kinds of libraries;[4] and 4) the Maryland
Manpower Project--with funds from the U. S. Office of Education, the National Science Foundation, and the National Library of Medicine--of which more will be said later.

    The role of librarianship is changing rapidly and man-
power needs are drastically affected by this change.   Many
articles, too numerous to mention here, support this argument.   Suffice it to say, as Harlow predicted, the full staffing of our libraries in the future will require radically over-
hauling the organization and responsibility of positions and
people. [5]   Both Tauber[6] and Wight support the need for behavioral research in the "almost untouched field of human
relations. "[7]   Yet relatively little has been done to date.

    This concept of human capital is actually an old one
in which interest has recently been revived.   Arguments still

rage concerning what is "professional" in librarianship. In
business and industry experimental research has been done
on such matters as working conditions and employee efficiency,
manager-employee relations, employee dissatisfaction, and
the social organization of employees. Many research studies
in such areas as status and power are being done in sociology. The concept of leadership studies and role playing--and
tests and measurements--are topics being explored by social
psychologists. In the social sciences, cross disciplinary ad-
vances are being made to formulate new methods of attacking
these administrative problems; leadership studies, communications theory and role theory are good examples. One com-
plaint, however, which is made by Mosher, is that at present
". . . there is inadequate communication between . . . related fields of the social sciences . . . there is inadequate
collaboration, cooperation and interaction among them. "[8]
Certainly research on librarianship could take advantage of
these possibilities and should not hesitate to take up the
challenge. What is needed is increased knowledge and understanding of how to accomplish objectives through people.
This is one important underlying issue which affects the ways
in which libraries function effectively. Library surveys give
no solution to the problem since they are, for the most part,
on the particular library being surveyed and only cover such
things as salaries and training of staff members. [9]

At this stage of sociological and socio-psychological
study of the library as a social system, only one group, the
library executive, has been isolated in his behavioral patterns and other characteristics. Probably the main reason
for concentration on administrators is that, unfortunately,
career advancement has always been tied to administration.
This is no longer necessarily true and will become less so

as the non-administrative librarian emerges as an important figure in the organization which has always been dominated by the personality of the executive. This emergence will come through actual service to the public by those who know a great deal about resources and how to satisfy the real needs of the public. It will become more evident as the progress of the library becomes more dependent upon the integration of the abilities of its members with physical resources and technology and management. Studies have confirmed that there is direct relationship between the quality of human resources engaged in management and the productivity of employees. [10] There seems to be fairly general agreement on the qualities that this group of librarians should possess. McDiarmid lists three important factors in the development of library leaders: personal qualities, proper education, and adequate experience. [11] Other studies of the executive have, likewise, focused on the three categories: mental, personal, and physical. The results have been, as could be expected, to establish the fact that there are all kinds of executives in libraries.

One such study, which focused on the unique personality characteristics of library administrators, used a personality inventory as a basis for concluding that the academic librarian is highly intelligent and self-assured, but lacks initiative. [12] Attempts to show how librarians differ from other professionals in similar fields are not so conclusive, particularly since individuals with a wide range of personalities and abilities do find success in this occupation. These studies[13, 14, 15] explore the background, status, and education of library executives and do little more than enumerate age, sex, salary, marital status, etc. However, these studies have identified certain individual qualifications that

may result in successful leadership ability. Certainly one
conclusion that may be drawn from the data presented is that
the administrative group seems to wear the halo, as measured
by salaries. A review, by Pollard,[16] using the ethnic background as a variable, found significant differences in age
(older) and education (less) of the black executives as compared to the white executives in libraries. Factual data of
this nature is important to provide effective long range planning and to take advantage of developing opportunities, particularly since so many of the top administrators in the profession are reaching retirement age.

On a more personal basis, organizational effectiveness is, in large measure, dependent upon the capacity of
those who direct the organization. Leadership traits, as
mentioned before, are a crucial ingredient in this type of
investigation and have been used to determine the informal
relations which exist among librarians in an attempt to up-
grade the level of library service.[17] In exploring the social,
economic, demographic, and other characteristics of public
library executives, Nash found the dominant characteristic
among them to be their acceptance of professional theory and
practice, but he was not able successfully to relate other
factors. However, he left little doubt that increasing emphasis is on administrative ability coupled with adroitness in
human relations and communications skills. A similar study,
done in 1939,[18] attempted to determine whether the amount
of previous education, experience and training had any affect
on the rate and extent of professional advancement, and what
correlation there was between that and certain other variables. The study concluded that administrators owed their
advancement to intangible factors and qualities which do not
permit easy measurement. An interesting sidelight revealed

in this study was that a majority of the chief librarians
queried had entered the library profession before reaching
the age of twenty-five, and one in six had had full-time work
experience in another professional field before shifting to librarianship. However, Harvey[19] found the average age of
public librarians to be twenty-four years, and one-third of
those he queried had had another position before coming into
the profession. He also maintained that personal character-
istics--sex, marital status, education and experience--influ-
enced the selection of a chief librarian. Such studies, although contradictory on some points, have enumerated factors
most important in providing motivation and satisfaction.

There is no evidence that this research has yielded
useful results. As far as this writer can determine, there
has been no significant improvement in our ability or efforts
to predict who will rise faster or who will make better library administrators. As a companion to these studies, it
would seem that future research would be profitable in the
study of sub-groups in the library, as a means toward find-
ing out the combinations of executive roles that constitute
viable groups. Just such an investigation, of the attitudes
and behavior toward change of administrators of large libraries, is now going on at Maryland.[20] The study has as its
purpose the analysis of selection, choice, and advancement
of those in administrative positions in libraries.

There is a growing awareness that the study of leadership cannot be adequately conducted without reference to the
cultural situation in which that leadership takes place. This
trend is part of a general shift away from the traditional
psychological "trait" approach, in favor of an approach which
stresses situational variation in leadership. This trend is
emphasized in the works of Farley and Michelson. Farley,[21]

in his research on the executive as an individual, identified
certain patterns in the ways in which he responded to administrative problems.   His findings--marked differences between the administrative patterns of the head librarians of
public libraries and head librarians of academic libraries--
reveal that the public librarian is the more scientific administrator.   Another conclusion he draws is that all administrators tend, generally, to neglect public relations in
libraries.   Where does this leave us in relation to the library's public?   The client relationship is a central role of
any professional, his raison d'être.

Knapp maintains that the academic library administrator, for instance, unless he teaches or does research,
may find that what status he has is derived almost completely
from his university's administrative status system.   To gain
respect the librarian must know his faculty and administration, their interests, their research problems, their professional commitments, and their students.   Most faculty
are likely to express more respect if the librarian's background, education, skills, and experience are comparable to
their own.   Knapp concludes that the

> college librarian has an anomalous status in the
> college.   In his competition with his faculty col-
> leagues, he is hampered by the fact that his own
> profession is relatively low in status.   And he is
> further hampered by the fact that the part of his
> training which is distinctively recognizable as li-
> brarianship is unimpressive . . . If he is in fact
> a bookman or an educator, he is sometimes as-
> sumed to be so not because of, but almost in spite
> of his library training. [22]

Unfortunately, her observations are based on personal im-
pressions and experiences, as are too many of the others in
the literature, and not on established facts or research.

One researcher, following Miss Knapp's approach, is attempting to determine the major areas of agreement and disagreement in regard to the expected role of the librarian in academic libraries. [23] Because of the tremendous pressures, many in conflict with each other, which exist in universities and colleges, conflicts arise between librarians and the faculty and administration. The librarian's potential contribution to the university has not been fully realized. "The librarian's contribution to the educational task of the college is still more potential than actual. There is a need for the administrator and the instructor to accept the librarian as an intellectual equal and practicing partner. "[24]

The chief librarian in public libraries and his relationship to groups external to the library has also been explored. Carpenter[25] found the relationships of the administrators and trustees not clearly defined, and tension between the two common. None of these studies, unfortunately, explore the differential prestige associated with the specific position of the library executive, an occupation having characteristics of both professional and executive positions. This, then, is the current state of research on the library administrator.

Manpower studies on other types of librarians are much less frequent. Personality and ability patterns of librarians and prospective librarians have been sought in a few psychological and sociological studies, in addition to the ones which investigate the academic background and the educational content needed to fit individuals for careers in librarianship. On the topic of recruitment, several papers have hypothesized that the image of an occupation is an important factor in recruitment to it. Accordingly, potential recruits match their characteristics against those of the image and are attracted or repelled by what they find.

Several studies seem to indicate the possibilities that
the stereotyped conception of occupational personality and
character may be strong mechanisms of recruitment to librarianship. Reagan[26] found five factors chiefly responsible
for influencing students to become librarians: other individuals, publicity of the profession, use of libraries, work experience in libraries, and library education. From these
she identified individual librarians as the key factor in influencing students to become librarians. On the other hand,
Ryan[27] maintained that recruitment of potential candidates to
librarianship was most likely to take place among college
students who had had satisfying experiences as users of academic and public libraries. More data is needed to properly
evaluate the recruitment possibilities because too much of
the approach to recruitment has been cursory and often un-
successful. Obviously good paper records, high intelligence
scores and scholastic marks are not sufficient for entrance
into graduate programs.

Contrary to studies done in other professions, Douglas, [28] in exploring the general importance of personality
structure, found that the behavior patterns of librarians have
been established before entering library school. This is
contrary to other studies because in recent decades other
disciplines, notably anthropology, psychology and sociology,
have supplied new insight into the nature of human personality
and behavior. It is now realized that people can be trained
to influence one another in desirable directions, to communicate better, and to understand each other more fully, and
various professions are becoming preoccupied with the nature
of human behavior. A current problem in recruitment is the
need to begin to shift the balance in the educational back-

grounds--and consequently the behavior--of those who function as librarians.

Establishing the validity of personality tests is extremely difficult. However, most writers agree that the personal traits which promote success in librarianship are the same ones that contribute to success in similar professions. Personality profile inventories have been used to describe characteristics of public librarians. [29] The study, done in the early 1950's, concluded that librarians, as a group, identify with the genteel, bookish, aesthetic tradition and that their preferences and special knowledges are in the fields of literature, languages, history, art and the humanities, generally, rather than in the scientific, technological, and politico-economic specialities and concerns of the day. The emphasis now being given to the need for specialists in science information and documentation work would probably have a significant effect on such a study done today. It would seem, more and more, that persons of very different characteristics, subject interests, and capacities for leadership are functioning in libraries today.

Along this same line of interests and motivations, Stone[30] identifies factors which encourage or discourage librarians from continuing their professional education and development once they take library jobs. Her findings confirm that administrators have a major responsibility to create conditions that are conducive to professional development. These conditions are slow in coming.

Plate,[31] who studied middle management in university libraries, found that specialists in those libraries alternate between librarianship and teaching. His observations were that the specialist regards himself more as a specialist than a librarian and that, generally, he is not interested in seek-

ing higher administrative positions toward which other middle
managers are motivated.

One other report, statistical in nature, is concerned
with characteristics of librarians. Schiller's study, [32] directed toward decision-making at the national level on manpower problems in college and university libraries, describes
the characteristics of professional personnel. Of pertinence
here are her findings that one-quarter of the sample have
graduate degrees in other fields, usually in addition to library degrees, and that eight percent of the sample cited
foreign languages as their primary activity.

Trumpeter, [33] in a smaller report, used the data base
collected by Schiller and made a study of academic library
professional employees who identified themselves as other-
than-librarians. She found little difference in salary, position level, or career satisfaction among them compared to
the professional librarians.

Finally, two other studies currently in the research state in the Maryland Manpower Project are the
Segal[34] study, which will be a comparative analysis of
librarianship with other professions (portions of that
study will probably duplicate Stone and Reagan since it
is to describe the characteristics which relate to the
choice of librarianship as a career, as well as the type
of library work involved), and the Presthus[35] study,
which is an effort to identify the structural and behavioral characteristics associated with organizational innova-
tion in libraries.

Need for this Study

It is evident that an assessment and honest evaluation

of the ways in which human beings are utilized in libraries is long overdue. If librarianship is to advance, then the organizations within which librarians function must be responsive in human and organizational terms to the restructuring of the field and of its practice. The tension in the relationship between librarians and their work environment, involving technological, organizational, and professional dimensions, must be recognized and controlled. Under these terms, it is important to understand the internal aspects of the library as a social system by exploring such questions as organization, task specialization, patterns of authority, relations, morale, and career expectations, which make up the environment within which librarians function.

There are many professional-specialist groups now working in libraries. Librarians themselves are placing greater emphasis upon establishing such specialized staffs who are able to tie the library to the developing programs of the university. These professional-specialists are causing changes in the make-up of the organization and relationships within that organization. One specialist who has emerged because of these demands is the area specialist bibliographer. Although during the development period of promoting and planning non-Western studies, no attention was given to qualifications of staff for processing and servicing library materials, the need for training librarians with the necessary area, subject, and language competencies would seem to be fairly obvious. [36]

In point of fact there was no general concept of what an area specialist bibliographer really was and what his place in the organization should be. Some persons filling the positions were inadequately prepared for their assignments. The organization of the resources as well as the relationship of

the library with the teaching faculty suffered because of this.
Even today there still is no agreement on the role of the
area bibliographer in academic libraries, [37] although most
writers agree on the need for the position. Many have expressed a need for role definitions:

> A very careful study of the role and status of a
> subject specialist within the library is overdue. [38]

> I suggest that we need to look very carefully at
> the role of the subject specialist--particularly the
> area specialist, the curator of a collection that has
> no home of its own--within the general library. [39]

> Another point requiring early attention is the defi-
> nition of the role of the area-studies librarian in
> the library and his status in the academic com-
> munity. [40]

Some would argue that the area bibliographer, because
of his assumed responsibility for book selection and for co-
ordinating library-related activities, has caused faculty to
have a different attitude toward librarians. "Such changes
[should have] heralded an even greater liaison between the
librarian and the scholar . . ."[41] If this is true it has
never been documented. Within the library itself, bibliographers' responsibilities are breaking down the traditional lines
between technical services and public services and this, too,
is causing change within the organization.

As a result of all of this it seems obvious that an
attempt to determine the place that area studies will have in
the academic libraries in the future, as related to collection
policies, faculty influence, and library organization, might
be an important step in analyzing the influence of area studies
on library operations. As was pointed out by one writer,

> Much more research needs to be done on the prob-
> lems inherent in the development of non-Western li-

brary resources--their selection, acquisition, the
servicing--and in the training of personnel . . .
A careful analysis of the experiences of established
centers should result in the definition of guidelines
applicable to new and changing programs. [42]

The area specialist bibliographer was chosen as the

subject of inquiry because he holds a key position in the li-

brary; his thinking and behavior influence the attitudes, values

and behavior of faculty, library administrators, and fellow

employees.   Complete lack of previous research in this area

justifies a rigorous study of his role.   The rationale for

this approach was derived from a framework suggested by

role theory.

The concept of role has assumed a key position in
the fields of sociology, social psychology, and
cultural anthropology.   Students of the social sciences frequently make use of it as a certain term
in conceptual schemes for the analysis of the structure and functioning of social systems and for the
explanation of individual behavior. [43]

Such an approach should enable one to develop a recommend-

ed model designed to eliminate present difficulties and am-

biguities and to improve administrative procedures for future

development of area programs.   This can be accomplished

by giving some indication of the climate of opinion toward

area specialist bibliographers and by isolating factors which

influence these opinions.   These bibliographers primarily

serve the specialized graduate area programs which are far

more developed and articulated than undergraduate general-

education courses and pose far more difficult and serious

problems for the library. [44]   These graduate programs are

centers of scholarship that have as their main aim the funda-

mental understanding of societies and cultures as a challeng-

ing and satisfying intellectual activity.   For these reasons

and because the members of the Association of Research Libraries represent the largest segment of the universities
which have advanced programs in area studies, it seems
appropriate to use these institutions as the universe for this
study. While it is true that several other colleges and universities do have area programs, these are mostly on the
undergraduate level and the majority are simply language
problems funded by the National Defense Education Act. The
limitations of this research, then, are those which are represented by choosing the definable population of ARL member institutions.

Since the normative survey method used in this study
relies heavily on sociological role theory, the following definitions should assist the reader in reviewing the conclusions
which the study presents:

Area specialist bibliographer: A specialist within the
library who spends all of his time working with area ma-
terials--whether this time is spent in selection, acquisition,
reference, or consulting with other technical services per-
sonnel--but whose primary responsibility is in the selection
and evaluation of the area collection.

Area Studies: An integrated, cross-disciplinary ap-
proach to a geographic area of the world. These studies
involve the geographical areas of Russia and Eastern Europe,
Latin America, the Far East, the Middle East, South and
Southeast Asia, and Africa. Non-Western studies has been
used interchangeably, by some authorities, with area studies.
The disciplines most often involved are History, Political
Science, Economics, Anthropology and Social Anthropology,
Ethnography and Ethnology, Geography, Sociology, International Relations, Philology and Linguistics, and Languages
and Literature.

Attitude: The individual's organization of psychological processes, as inferred from his behavior, with respect to some aspect of the world.[45]

Opinion: A judgment, conviction, view, or belief held by a person on some issue.[46]

Role: Represents the behavior expected of the occupant of a given position or status. In this definition two features are emphasized: 1) expectations (i. e., beliefs, cognitions) held by certain persons in regard to what behaviors are appropriate for the occupant of a given position; and 2) enactments (i. e., conduct) of a person who is assigned to, or selected to enter, a given position.[47]

Role adequacy: Background, biographical data of the person in the role being considered[48]--in this case the area specialist bibliographer.

Role expectation: Actions or qualities expected of the occupant of a position; when viewed as actions, role expectations are codified as in a job description; when viewed as qualities, role expectations are coded in verbal terms.[49]

Role perception: Similar to role expectation except that perception is one's own view of his own role while expectation is usually associated with what others expect. Role perception was used interchangeably in this study with role expectation, depending on who's view was being expressed. If it was the bibliographer's view, the term perception was used; if it was the faculty or administrator's view, the term expectation was used. Role performance depends on a person's perception of his role.[50]

Role strain: Comes largely from failure of certain processes to function adequately, so as to leave unclear, incomplete, and contradictory elements in a role. This may come about through failure of role clues, lack of role consensus, etc. This strain need not be undesirable. [51]

To gather the information for the main part of this
study, 362 questionnaires were sent to area specialist bibliographers, library administrators, and faculty teaching in
area study programs in ARL institutions. Almost 75 per
cent of them responded and it is on those responses, plus
the responses solicited through a number of personal inter-
views, that the remainder of this study is based.

Notes

1. Maurice F. Tauber, "Measurement and Evaluation of
    Research in Library Technical Services," in Research
    Methods in Librarianship: Measurement and Evalua-
    tion, ed. by Herbert Goldhor (Champaign, Illinois:
    University of Illinois, Graduate School of Library Sci-
    ence, 1967), p. 116.

2. Libraries at Large, ed. by Douglas M. Knight and E.
    Shepley Nourse (New York: R. R. Bowker Co. , 1969)
    p. 167.

3. David Kaser, "Dispelling Hunches, Intuitions, and Pro-
    fessional Mystique," Wilson Library Bulletin, XLI,
    No. 9 (May, 1967), 923-25.

4. Lester Asheim, "Library Activities in the Field of Man-
    power, 1967," in Conference on Library Manpower
    Needs and Utilization, ed. by Lester Asheim (Chicago
    American Library Association, 1967).

5. Neal Harlow, "The Present is Not What It Was," Li-
    brary Journal, LXXXIX (June 15, 1964), 2527-32.

6. Maurice F. Tauber, "Introduction," Library Trends, VI
    (October, 1967), 107.

7. Edward A. Wight, "Research in Organization and Ad-
    ministration," Library Trends, VI (October, 1957),
    145.

8. F. C. Mosher, "Research in Public Administration:
    Some Notes and Suggestions," Public Administration

Review, XVI (1956), 178.

9. Lowell A. Martin, "Personnel in Library Surveys," in Library Surveys, ed. by M. F. Tauber and L. R. Stephens (New York: Columbia University Press, 1967), p. 138.

10. Frederick Horbison and Charles A. Myers, "The Logic of Management Development," in Management of Human Resources, ed. by Paul Pigors, C. A. Myers, and F. T. Marlin (New York: McGraw-Hill, 1964).

11. E. W. McDiarmid, "The Place of Experience in Developing College and University Librarians," Library Quarterly, XII, No. 3 (July, 1942), 614-21.

12. Perry D. Morrison, "The Career of the Academic Librarian" (unpublished DLS dissertation, School of Librarianship, University of California, Berkeley, 1960).

13. B. W. Bradley, "Study of the Characteristics, Qualifications, and Succession Patterns of Heads of Large United States Academic and Public Libraries" (unpublished Master's thesis, Graduate School of Library Science, University of Texas, 1968).

14. L. F. Zimmerman, "The Academic and Professional Education of College and University Librarians" (unpublished Master's thesis, Graduate School of Library Science, University of Illinois, 1932).

15. Chalmers Davidson, "The Status of the Librarian in Southern Liberal Arts Colleges" (unpublished Master's thesis, Graduate Library School, University of Chicago, 1936).

16. Frances M. Pollard, "Characteristics of Negro College Chief Librarians," College and Research Libraries, XXV, No. 4 (July, 1964), 281-84.

17. William V. Nash, "Characteristics of Administrative Heads of Public Libraries in Various Communications Categories" (unpublished Ph. D. dissertation, Graduate School of Library Science, University of Illinois, 1964).

18. Robert Smyth Alvarez, "Qualifications of Heads of Li-

braries in Cities of Over Ten Thousand Population in
the Seven North-Central States" (unpublished Ph. D.
dissertation, Graduate Library School, University of
Chicago, 1939).

19. John F. Harvey, "Variety in the Experience of Chief
    Librarians. " College and Research Libraries, XIX,
    No. 2 (March, 1958), 107-10.

20. This project, coordinated by Paul Wasserman and Mary
    Lee Bundy, is being funded by the U. S. Office of Ed-
    ucation and sponsored by the University of Maryland
    School of Library and Information Services.   It is
    titled Leadership for Change.

21. Richard Alan Farley, "The American Library Executive:
    An Inquiry into His Concepts of the Functions of His
    Office, " (unpublished Ph. D. dissertation, Graduate
    School of Library Science, University of Illinois,
    1967).

22. Patricia B. Knapp, "The College Librarian: Sociology
    of a Professional Specialization, " College and Re-
    search Libraries, XVI, No. 1 (January, 1955), 71.

23. Aaron Michelson, "The Academic Librarian" (Ph. D. dis-
    sertation in progress, Graduate Library School, Uni-
    versity of Chicago).

24. Henry Howard Scherer, "Faculty-Librarian Relationships
    in Selected Liberal Arts Colleges" (unpublished Ed. D.
    dissertation, School of Education, University of South-
    ern California, 1960), p. 36.

25. Raymond Leonard Carpenter, "The Public Library Ex-
    ecutive: A Study of Status and Role" (unpublished
    Ph. D. dissertation, University of North Carolina,
    1968).

26. Agnes Lytton Reagan, "A Study of Certain Factors in
    Institutions of Higher Education Which Influence Stu-
    dents to Become Librarians" (unpublished Ph. D. dis-
    sertation, Graduate School of Library Science, Uni-
    versity of Illinois, 1957).

27. Mary Jane Ryan, "Career Development of Librarians, "
    Minnesota Libraries, XXII, No. 6 (Summer, 1968),
    174-78.

28. Robert Raymond Douglas, "The Personality of the Librarian" (unpublished Ph. D. dissertation, Graduate Library School, University of Chicago, 1957).

29. Alice L Bryan, "Public Librarians: A Study of Professional Personnel in the American Public Library," in The Public Library Inquiry, ed. by Robert D. Leigh et. al. (Chicago: Chicago University Press, 1950).

30. Elizabeth W. Stone, Factors Related to the Professional Development of Librarians (Metuchen, New Jersey: Scarecrow Press, 1969).

31. Kenneth Harry Plate, "Middle Management in University Libraries: The Development of a Theoretical Model for Analysis" (unpublished Ph. D. dissertation, Rutgers University, Graduate School of Library Service, 1969).

32. Anita R. Schiller, Characteristics of Professional Personnel in College and University Libraries (Springfield: Illinois State Library, 1969).

33. Margo Trumpeter, "Non-Librarians in the Academic Library," College and Research Libraries, XXIX, No. 6 (November, 1968), 461-65.

34. Stanley J. Segal, "Personality and Ability Patterns of Library and Information Service Workers Related to Work Roles and Work Settings," (research in progress at School of Library and Information Services, University of Maryland).

35. Robert Presthus, "The Librarian's Role in a Changing Organization: A Case Approach," (research in progress at School of Library and Information Services, University of Maryland).

36. Richard D. Lambert. ed. , Resources for South Asian Area Studies in the United States (Philadelphia: University of Pennsylvania Press, 1962), p. 104.

37. See particularly: Robert P. Haro, "The Bibliographer in the Academic Library," Library Resources and Technical Services, XIII, No. 2 (Spring, 1969), 163-69; Helen Welch Tuttle, "An Acquisitionist Looks at Mr. Haro's Bibliographer," Library Resources and

Technical Services, XIII, No. 2 (Spring, 1969), 170-74; Cecil K. Byrd, "Subject Specialists in a University Library, " College and Research Libraries, XXVII, No. 3 (May, 1966), 191-93.

38. Louis A. Jacob, "South Asian Area Studies and the Library: Discussion," Library Quarterly, XXXV, No. 4 (October, 1965), 238.

39. Ibid. , 237.

40. Howard W. Winger, "Education for Area Studies Librarianship," Library Quarterly, XXXV, No. 4 (October, 1965), 370.

41. Paul L. Berry, "Development of Library Resources," in The Non-Western World in Higher Education, ed. by Donald N. Bigelow and Lyman Legters (Philadelphia: American Academy of Political and Social Sciences, 1964), p. 128.

42. Philip J. McNiff, "Foreign Area Studies and Their Effect on Library Development," College and Research Libraries, XXIV, No. 4 (July, 1963), 305.

43. Neal Gross, et. al. , Explorations in Role Analysis (New York: John Wiley and Sons, Inc. , 1966), p. 3.

44. Chauncy D. Harris, "Area Studies and Library Resources," Library Quarterly, XXXV, No. 4 (October, 1965), 206.

45. Julius Gould and William L. Kolb, eds. , A Dictionary of the Social Sciences, (New York: The Free Press, 1964), p. 40.

46. Ibid. , p. 477.

47. David L. Sills, ed. , International Encyclopedia of the Social Sciences, (New York: The Macmillan Co. , 1968), v. XII, p. 546.

48. Ibid. , p. 555.

49. Ibid. , p. 547.

50. Ibid. , p. 546.

51. Ibid. , p. 556.

Chapter III

THE AREA SPECIALIST BIBLIOGRAPHER'S PROFILE DEVELOPMENT AND ITS INFLUENCE ON EXPECTATIONS

Introduction

Some authorities assert, in career development theory, that one's work role is an expression of one's personal characteristics, as well as one's personality and needs.[1] In planning a study of area specialist bibliographers it seemed relevant and desirable to gain a better understanding of the profession by examining whether these theories may apply to the area bibliographer group. This group of men and women is responsible in large measure for the development of library collections in the "areas." Preceding chapters have shown their emergence in the evolution of the area concept.

A portion of the questionnaire used in this study was designed to permit accumulation of certain data bearing on background variables of the area bibliographer, since these variables probably have great influence on the expectations of the faculty and administrators toward the bibliographer's fulfillment of his role.

Detailed characteristics of the man himself, which may influence the extent to which he acts according to role expectations, are presented here. Of the total of 126 area specialist bibliographers serving ARL libraries, 30 are profiled in this section of the study. To present a clearer picture of the area bibliographer and to further validate the

representativeness of the sample, a "control" group of area
bibliographers was drawn from biographical directories. [2]
This control group includes 37 area specialist bibliographers.
Therefore, when certain variables are discussed in this section, comparisons are made between the original 30 in the
sample population and the 37 in the control group.

Sex

One general thesis is that "in every society, from
primitive to modern, sex is important in the selection and
allocation of occupations. "[3]   Some studies have found that in
times of shortage of professional workers, the sexes may
inflitrate each other's world. [4]   Frequently, sex determines
whether an individual is given consideration for a particular
position.   Whether or not sex is a role factor for the area
bibliographer position was not considered in this study; how-
evcr, the position does not appear to be sex oriented.

Females constitute about one-third, 32 percent, of the
total population of area bibliographers.   This ratio is comparable to that of other studies which have been done on sex
ratios in all technical and professional occupations.   One
such report indicated that 38 percent of all positions in these
occupations are held by women. [5]   Schiller, on the other
hand, found that 64 percent of all academic librarians in her
survey were women, [6] and Harvey's survey likewise indicates
that females dominate the college library field; 60 percent
of his sample were female. [7]   Table 1 on the following page
shows the sex ratio of area bibliographers by area program.

Education

The educational background of the area bibliographer

TABLE 1

SEX RATIO OF AREA BIBLIOGRAPHERS BY PROGRAM*
(By Frequency and by Per Cent)

PROGRAM	MALE		FEMALE		TOTAL	
	Sample (n=22)	Population (n=86)	Sample (n=8)	Population (n=40)	Sample (n=30)	Population (n=126)+
African	4(13.332%)	7(5.55%)	1(3.333%)	4(3.19%)	5(16.66%)	11(8.73%)
East Asian	4(13.332%)	21(16.66%)	1(3.333%)	7(5.55%)	5(16.66%)	28(22.22%)
Latin American	1(3.335%)	12(9.52%)	2(6.666%)	14(11.11%)	3(10.0%)	26(20.63%)
Middle Eastern	3(9.999%)	9(7.14%)	1(3.333%)	4(3.19%)	4(13.33%)	13(10.33%)
Russian and East European	6(20.008%)	23(18.25%)	3(9.999%)	8(6.35%)	9(30.02%)	31(24.60%)
South and South-east Asian	4(13.332%)	14(11.11%)	0(--)	3(2.38%)	4(13.33%)	17(13.49%)
TOTAL	22(73.336%)	86(68.0%)	8(26.664%)	40(32.0%)	30(100%)	126(100%)

*Total sex ratio of all programs is given here because this information was easily obtainable from the original letter response which came from Personnel Librarians in ARL institutions.
+Some of the 109 programs with area bibliographers have more than one bibliographer serving the program.

is a matter of importance because his basic qualifications
should have bearing on attitudes.   One of the best indications
of the professional stature of the area bibliographer is revealed by the type of degrees he has earned.

The general level of graduate training of area bibliographers is very high.   Thirteen percent of the sample have
completed their doctoral degree.   Only two of the sample
have gone no further than the bachelor's degree but both of
those have foreign training equivalent to the master's degree
in library science.   Five have degrees in area studies on the
bachelor's level and four on the master's level, 30 percent
of the sample have Area Studies degrees.   In addition, 73. 3
percent have library degrees.   Upon examination of the subjects in which the area bibliographers concentrated during
their formal training, a strong "major" concentration in two
disciplines, other than Area Studies, becomes evident.   These
two subjects common to the three degree levels are Languages and Literature, and History.   On the bachelor's level
these account for 54. 78 percent of the degrees; for 57. 69
percent on the master's level, and for 64. 28 percent on the
doctoral level.   The remaining degrees appear to be scattered
among a group of other subjects.

These findings are similar to those of other national
surveys of librarians, except that in the present study Area
Studies has replaced English and Journalism in the top three
categories.   Schiller reported the major fields of study for
the bachelor's degree, of all academic librarians in her
sample, were English and Journalism, with 29. 8 percent;
History, with 15. 2 percent; and Foreign Languages and Literature, with 10. 1 percent, [8] while Douglas found the major
fields were Literature, 35. 8 percent; History, 14. 4 percent;
and Foreign Languages, 10. 7 percent. [9]

TABLE 2

RANK ORDER OF MAJOR SUBJECTS ON THE BACHELORS LEVEL

Subject	Sample Group (n=30)		Control Group (n=37)		Combined Groups (n=67)	
	Rank	Percentage	Rank	Percentage	Rank	Percentage
Language and Literature	1	25. 0	1	39. 27	1	33. 87
History	2	20. 83	2	21. 05	2	20. 97
Area Studies	3	16. 67	4	5. 26	3	9. 68
English	4	8. 33	3	7. 89	4	7. 06
Education	4	8. 33	4	5. 26	5	6. 55
Political Science	4	8. 33	-	--	6	3. 33
Philosophy and Religion	-	--	4	5. 26	6	3. 33
Economics	-	--	4	5. 26	6	3. 33
Sociology	-	--	4	5. 26	6	3. 33
Anthropology	5	4. 17	-	--	7	1. 71
Classics	5	4. 17	-	--	7	1. 71
Library Science	5	4. 17	-	--	7	1. 71
International Development	-	--	5	2. 73	7	1. 71
Science	-	--	5	2. 73	7	1. 71
TOTAL		100%		100%		100%

Others have drawn conclusions concerning the handi-
caps of undergraduate education with majors in the humanities, including foreign languages. [10] However, librarians in
this study do have undergraduate majors in Languages and
Literature, which is advantageous to bibliographers because
they work with languages (see Table 2.)

Fourteen of the sample have two master's degrees,
three have two master's and a doctorate, and one subject in
the sample has three master's degrees, one of those being
in library science.   Twenty-three percent have master's degrees in library science but no subject masters and 16. 6
percent have subject masters but no library degree.   It might
be assumed that "there would be fewer [persons whose specialist talents may be said to dominate his talents as a li-
brarian] with training in both the specialty and in librarianship"[11] but this is not supported in this study.   Fifty-two
subjects in the combined group, about four-fifths, have degrees in library science.   This is slightly less than the five-
sixths of Schiller's population which had at least the first
professional degree. [12]

One may ask, with the strong subject emphasis, if
possession of a library degree is absolutely necessary for an
area bibliographer.   Perhaps a comment from a faculty member is pertinent here:

> In my field, knowledge of languages and subjects
> is worth much more than a library degree.   (Lan-
> guage Professor)

An interesting comparison can be made between the
present study and that done by Morrison.   Morrison found
that 58 percent of the males in his sample held a subject
master's degree while only 26 percent of the females did.
He hypothesized that "part of the advantage attributed to the

TABLE 3
RANK ORDER OF MAJOR SUBJECTS ON THE MASTERS LEVEL*

SUBJECT	SAMPLE GROUP (n=30)		CONTROL GROUP (n=37)		COMBINED GROUP (n=67)	
	Rank	Percentage	Rank	Percentage	Rank	Percentage
Language and Literature	1	52.381	1	36.688	1	42.308
Area Studies	3	9.523	2	23.333	2	19.231
History	2	14.286	3	16.668	3	15.385
Education	2	14.286	-	--	4	5.769
Political Science	-	--	4	6.666	5	3.846
Administration	4	4.762	-	--	6	1.923
Art/Art History	4	4.762	-	--	6	1.923
Anthropology	-	--	5	3.333	6	1.923
Economics	-	--	5	3.333	6	1.923
Journalism	-	--	5	3.333	6	1.923
Philosophy/Religion	-	--	5	3.333	6	1.923
Sociology	-	--	5	3.333	6	1.923
TOTAL		100%		100%		100%

*Excludes degrees in Library Science which have been discussed in text.

TABLE 4

RANK ORDER OF MAJOR SUBJECTS ON THE DOCTORAL LEVEL

SUBJECT	SAMPLE GROUP (n=4)		CONTROL GROUP (n=10)		COMBINED GROUP (n=14)	
	Rank	Percentage	Rank	Percentage	Rank	Percentage
Language and Literature	1	50.0	1	40.0	1	42.85
History	2	25.0	2	20.0	2	21.45
Political Science	2	25.0	-	--	3	7.14
Geography	-	--	3	10.0	3	7.14
Philosophy/Religion	-	--	3.	10.0	3	7.14
Law	-	--	3	10.0	3	7.14
Library Science	-	--	3	10.0	3	7.14
TOTAL		100%		100%		100%

degree may actually be due to the fact that men hold it more frequently than women and the men have an advantage simply because they are men. "[13] The present study differs drastically in the ratio of females; 50 percent hold the subject master's in addition to the library science degree. Perhaps this variance is due to the strong emphasis on subject backgrounds for all area bibliographers (see Table 3.)

On the doctoral level Language and Literature, and History, again, outranked all other disciplines and accounted for almost two-thirds of all the doctoral degrees. Four of the sample have obtained doctoral degrees. Fourteen, 20.89 percent of the combined group, have doctorates. This is much higher than Schiller's proportion of all academic librarians holding doctorates: 3.6 percent of her sample. [14] Another great difference in her findings and those of this study is that nearly 40 percent of her respondents, at the doctoral level, majored in History or Education. Table 4 shows that by far the greatest number of doctorates possessed by area bibliographers is in Languages and Literature, with History being the second largest discipline.

Only one bibliographer in the control group, and none of those in the sample group, has a doctorate in Library Science. Perhaps one of the reasons that library science is not strongly represented at this level is that most Ph. D. 's in Library Science have either assumed administrative posts or are teaching in library schools. This conclusion would support Danton's contention that librarians with Ph. D. 's in librarianship tend to gravitate to the higher administrative posts. [15]

Concerning educational qualifications of area bibliographers, the reactions of some faculty, library administrators, and bibliographers are summarized in the following comments:

> The area specialist librarian, like other librarians,
> is also and above all an information specialist.
> (Sociology Professor)

> The bibliographer's preparation has to be in the
> bibliography of the area.   This is his 'specialty.'
> If he's a specialist in Chinese ink-stones or Ch'ing
> Dynasty bureaucracy, he's apt to be more of a
> problem than a help.   (Language Professor)

> A librarian-bibliographer may well be trained in an
> academic discipline, but the chances of his own
> discipline being over-represented are fairly good.
> (Linguistics Professor)

> We used to say teachers who couldn't teach become
> librarians.   Now its librarians who can't do library
> work become area bibliographers.   (Administrator)

> The younger American trained specialist is usually
> qualified.   The older East European lawyer who is
> now doing this work is not necessarily well quali-
> fied.   (Anthropology Professor)

An analysis was performed to determine if, indeed, the possession of subject degrees had any bearing on the expectations of faculty and administrators toward the performance
of the area bibliographer.   No relationship was found between expectations on the part of the faculty and administrators and actual possession of higher degrees by the area
specialist bibliographer.

Again, it must be pointed out that expectations of the
faculty and administrators strongly supported the necessity
of subject knowledge by area bibliographers.   That this did
not relate to the actual possession of educational qualifications in a subject area could be interpreted as an indication
that, first, not enough qualified subject bibliographers were
available to fill the void which still exists in this area of li-

brarianship, or secondly, that the bibliographer's actual
knowledge of the area was not expressed in his formal education. At any rate, the following comments are indicative
of the strong feeling of the respondents to this point:

> I feel that the need is primarily for a bibliographer
> who is specialized in a discipline, with particular
> linguistic competence. (History Professor)
>
> The specialist bibliographer should be educated in
> much the same way as the faculty. (Bibliographer)
>
> The area specialist bibliographer should be as pre-
> pared as the faculty, educationally, but in different
> areas. (Economics Professor)
>
> Where the bibliographer has full control, his edu-
> cational background must be as good as any faculty
> member's--and as broad. (Administrator)

Languages Spoken

Eleven, 38 percent, of the sample and nine of the
control group speak five or more languages. German and
French are the two languages which are common to all areas.
Most, 66. 6 percent, of the Slavic and East European bibliographers in the sample speak all of the Slavic languages; in
addition, one other speaks both Russian and Polish. All of
the Latin American bibliographers in the sample speak Spanish and the majority also speak Portuguese. All of the East
Asian bibliographers speak both Japanese and Chinese; in addition, one speaks Korean. The majority, 75 percent, of
the Middle Eastern bibliographers in the sample speak both
Turkish and Arabic. The three South Asian bibliographers
in the sample speak Hindi, Bengali, and Urdu, and two of
them speak Sanskrit and Punjabi. In addition, one speaks
other Indic languages. The remaining bibliographer in the

TABLE 5

DISTRIBUTION OF LANGUAGES SPOKEN BY AREA BIBLIOGRAPHERS

LANGUAGE	AREA PROGRAMS						Total Both Groups
	African n=5 (n=6)	East Asian n=5 (n=6)	Latin American n=3 (n=11)	Middle Eastern n=4 (n=1)	Russian and East European n=9 (n=13)	South and Southeast Asian r=4 (n=4)	n=67
Spanish	2		3 (11)	1	(1)		18
Portuguese	3		2 (8)		(1)		14
Italian	1		(2)		(3)		6
Russian	1		(1)		9 (13)		24
Ukrainian			(1)		7 (8)		16
Bulgarian					6 (7)		13
Serbo-Croatian					6 (8)		14
Polish			(1)		8 (10)		19
Czech					7		7
Slovak					6		6
Latvian					1 (1)		2
Hungarian					1		1
Persian				1			1
Arabic				3 (1)			4
Greek					(1)		1
Turkish				3			3

							Total
German	5 (2)	1 (1)	1 (3)	2	4 (10)	1	30
French	5 (2)	1 (2)	3 (5)	2 (1)	4 (10)	1	36
Afrikaans	2						2
Dutch	2						2
Swahili	2						2
Yoruba	2						2
Hausa	1						1
Bantuguese	1						1
Chinese		5 (6)					11
Japanese		5 (4)					10
Korean		1 (1)					2
Sudanese						1	1
Urdu						3 (1)	4
Punjabi						2 (1)	3
Sanskrit						2 (1)	3
Hindi						3 (1)	4
Bengali						3	3
Marathi						1	1
Gujarati						1	1
Vietnamese						1	1
Indonesian						1	1
Burmese						(1)	1

*Control group is in parenthesis except in the Total column.

South and Southeast Asian group is oriented toward Southeast
Asia, being able to speak the major languages of that area
in addition to the colonial languages of French and Dutch.
The most interesting, though not startling, difference is
found in the African bibliographers, all of whom speak the
colonial languages of French and German. In addition, three
speak Portuguese and two speak Spanish and Afrikaans. The
only "native" languages represented in this group are Swahili,
Bantuguese, Hausa, and Yoruba.

A wide range of opinions was expressed on the language needs and abilities of area bibliographers. The following comments are typical of feelings which were expressed:

> Concerning the linguistic abilities of a bibliographer,
> some areas--at least as traditionally defined--are
> multi-lingual. The specialist bibliographer for
> each area cannot be expected to know all these
> languages. Perhaps such an area should be broken
> up into smaller sub-areas. (Professor of Religion)

> For the ancient Near East, a knowledge of the
> principal modern European Languages is more im-
> portant than a knowledge of any of the ancient lan-
> guages. The bibliographer should be largely guided
> by reviews by competent, judicious specialists. To
> know which reviewers are competent and judicious
> implies a well informed acquaintance with the field.
> (Professor of Religion)

> Language skills vary from area to area. In South
> Asia, for instance, certain programs could get
> along without any. But, on the whole, languages
> are important. (Bibliographer)

> In the case of the modern Near East, knowledge of
> at least two of the languages of the area is indis-
> pensable. (Professor of Religion)

> There are over 1,000 different languages of my
> area and I am quite happy to report that I do not
> speak one of them. It is important, however, to
> appreciate the fact that the area librarian is a

> specialist in the scholarly literature of the area.
> For my area this literature is in the languages of
> the former colonial powers and the languages of
> modern world scholarship. (Bibliographer)

Table 5 enumerates the languages spoken by the area bibli-

ographers.

The importance of possessing some knowledge of

foreign languages in the field of librarianship has been real-

ized for quite some time.   However, extensive or intensive

language proficiency was not of major concern until quite

recently, actually coinciding with the development of area

programs in academic libraries.   It is obvious that language

training is needed by those academic librarians who must

cope with the flood of materials in "exotic" languages.   The

need is becoming more acute as area programs continue to

grow.   Federal programs such as PL 480 and the National

Plan for Acquisition and Cataloging, in addition to the Farm-

ington Plan, Latin American Cooperative Acquisitions Pro-

gram, and others, have compounded the problem.

One of the unique problems with area studies was that

there was no one faculty member competent to select current

and retrospective materials in the vernacular languages.   This

is quite different from the "Western" programs which are in

existence.   As Wagman points out:

> The political scientist specializing in German poli-
> tical history and current affairs is often glad to do
> the book selection in his field.   He may even insist
> on doing it rather than leaving it to the librarians.
> His colleague in the political science department
> whose field is South Asia or Southeast Asia is more
> inclined to leave book selection to the library or
> even to require that it be done there. [16]

Over three-fourths, 77. 63 percent, of the respondents felt

that an area specialist bibliographer's working knowledge of

languages of the area was necessary. As one professor
maintained:

> The bibliographer should have a working knowledge
> of the main languages of publication, but not for
> all languages of the area.

This expectation, however, was independent of the actual
possession of the skill. Perhaps one of the reasons that
there was no relationship between the expectations concerning the knowledge of languages and the actual possession of
that skill was that the majority of the respondents expected
the bibliographer to have a working knowledge of the important languages of the "area. " Whether or not that particular bibliographer possessed these skills seemed to be ir-
relevant to the expectations.

Disciplines of Publication

        The theme of discipline specialization and emphasis
on Languages and Literature, and History is found to carry
over into the published works of area bibliographers. Almost three-fourths of the sample have published materials in
their area of interest. That library science is the major
area of publication is no surprise since one of the primary
activities of area bibliographers is making the whole public
aware, through the creation of bibliographies and other reference guides, of the resources available. Following Harvey's
observation that academic librarians are expected to publish, [17] the large majority of area bibliographers seem to
have accepted the responsibility. This present study sub-
stantiates the statement by Morrison that "publication is primarily a masculine phenomenon. "[18] A large majority, 86. 36
percent, of the male bibliographers in this sample have pub-

TABLE 6

DISCIPLINE OF RESEARCH IN ORDER OF FREQUENCY

DISCIPLINE	SAMPLE GROUP (n=30)		CONTROL GROUP (n=37)		COMBINED GROUP (n=67)	
	Frequency	Percentage	Frequency	Percentage	Frequency	Percentage
Library Science	7	26.92	17	65.382	24	46.16
History	8	30.76	4	15.384	12	23.08
Language and Literature	5	19.23	3	11.538	8	15.38
Anthropology/Archaeology	2	7.69	1	3.848	3	5.77
Area Studies	1	3.85	1	3.848	2	3.85
Art/Art History	1	3.85	-	---	1	1.92
Political Science	1	3.85	-	---	1	1.92
Humanities (other)	1	3.85	-	---	1	1.92
TOTAL		100%		100%		100%

lished some type of research while only 37.5 percent of the female area bibliographers have published.

It is certain, from the results shown in Table 6, that area bibliographers are among the most prolific writers in the library field. Whether or not this can be associated with the tendency to identify with faculty cannot be determined by this present study. However, many respondents feel that the "publish or perish" syndrome should carry over into librarianship. Some of the comments reflect mixed feelings. To the question: "In your opinion should the area specialist bibliographer be actively engaged in research or teaching in the area program," the following are typical comments:

> The bibliographer is . . . best qualified if engaged in research, but whether it is really necessary to have such a superman is hard to say. (History Professor)

> These people should participate in teaching and research in an academic department in a minimal way at least. (Administrator)

Visits to the "Area"

Eighty percent of the sample have visited their "area" for purposes other than family residence. Most of those, 62.5 percent, listed as their primary purpose for the visit as being buying missions for their libraries. In addition, a large number, 58.3 percent, listed study and research as their objectives in traveling to the "area." It is interesting to note that all of the African bibliographers have been on at least one buying trip to that area, while three of the East Asian bibliographers and two of the South and Southeast Asian bibliographers have been on buying trips to the "area" of responsibility. These trips are less frequent among other types

TABLE 7

PURPOSES OF VISITS TO "AREA" BY FREQUENCY

PURPOSE	AREA PROGRAMS						
	African (n=5)	East Asian (n=5)	Latin American (n=3)	Middle Eastern (n=4)	Russian and East European (n=9)	South and Southeast Asian (n=4)	Total (n=30)
Buying Trip	5	3	1	1	3	2	15
Family Residence	1	5	0	0	4	4	14
Research	2	2	1	0	3	3	11
Pleasure	3	1	2	1	3	0	10
Study	0	0	0	1	3	0	4
Business	0	1	0	1	1	0	3
U.S. Government	0	0	1	0	0	0	1
Foundation Sponsored	1	0	0	0	0	0	1
Military Service	0	0	0	1	0	0	1
International Mission	0	0	0	0	1	0	1

of bibliographers.   The trips ranged in length from two days
to five months, but averaged one month.   Most of those who
have been on buying or research trips have been at least
twice and several have been three or more times.   Table 7
indicates the purposes for all such visits.

There appears to be a clear pattern of repeated and/
or extended trips to one country, exclusively or in conjunc-
tion with relatively short trips to other "area" countries.
The language spoken by the individual almost always corres-
ponds to the country which he visited most frequently or for
the longest period of time.

Those visiting the "area" are most productive in their
research efforts.   In fact, those who visited the area on
buying trips are the most productive on the whole.   Forty
percent of all area bibliographers in this study have visited
the area on buying trips and have published in their area of
interest, while almost two-thirds of all bibliographers have
visited the area, whether on buying trips or for other reasons, and have published.

Country of Birth

Only two-fifths of the sampled area bibliographers
were born in the U. S.   This is expected since we have, for
many years, drawn on the talents and expertise of immigrant
librarians, particularly from East Europe and Asia.   This
figure differs drastically from Schiller's findings, that nine
out of ten were born in the U. S. [19]   Although it is not the
intent of this study to determine how many of the sample
were actually trained in foreign countries, it seems legitimate
to speculate from the data presented that the majority of
those who were born abroad took their library training in the
U. S.

TABLE 8
DISTRIBUTION OF RESPONDENTS BY PLACE OF BIRTH*

AREA PROGRAMS

PLACE OF BIRTH	African n=5(n=2)	East Asian n=5(n=6)	Latin American n=3(n=12)	Middle Eastern n=4(n=1)	Russian and East European n=9(n=12)	South and Southeast Asian n=4(n=4)	Total (Combined) n=30(n=37)
Argentina			(2)				2
China		4 (6)					10
Czechoslovakia					1		1
Egypt				(1)			1
Estonia					1		1
Hong Kong		1					1
India						2 (2)	4
Latvia			(1)				1
Mexico			(1)				1
Poland					1 (2)		3
Portugal			1 (1)				2
Puerto Rico			(1)				1
Russia					(1)		1
Ukraine					1 (3)		4
United Kingdom	3 (1)				1		5
United States	2 (1)		2 (6)	4	3 (5)	1 (2)	26
Yugoslavia					1 (1)		2

*Numbers in parenthesis represent the control group. Totals are for both the sample and the control groups.

Of those born outside the U.S., about three-fourths, 76.5 percent, came to this country between the ages of twenty and forty.

Professional and Scholarly
Association Membership

Affiliation with professional and scholarly associations is a factor of importance in a study of the personal characteristics of the area bibliographer. Such affiliations are an indication of the dominating interest of specialists. It is quite evident that area bibliographers feel it worthwhile to be members of professional and scholarly associations. All but one of the sample reported that they belong to a national library association or a national "area" association. About one-half, 52 percent, of the area bibliographers who possess library degrees are members of the American Library Association. Perhaps this low percentage is because ALA has not, until very recently, been "area" oriented. Granted, the Slavic and East European Sub-section of the ACRL section has been in existence for a few years, but it was the only area which was represented until the recent creation of the Asian and North African Sub-section.

The other associations cited indicate the interests of individual groups of area bibliographers. Whether association membership is necessarily beneficial to the libraries and to the bibliographers is questionable. The following remarks are representative of some who express skepticism as to the value of belonging to national associations:

> No one should think of attending national 'area' association meetings. (History Professor)

> I am anxious to maintain my position as an informed academic librarian . . . [however] in terms

TABLE 9

MEMBERSHIP IN PROFESSIONAL AND SCHOLARLY ASSOCIATIONS*

ASSOCIATIONS	AREA PROGRAM						
	African n=5	East Asian n=5	Latin American n=3	Middle Eastern n=4	Russian and East European n=9	South and Southeast Asian n=4	Total n=30
"AREA" ASSOCIATIONS							
African Studies Assn.	5						5
International African Inst.	2						2
Assn. for Asian Studies		5				2	7
Latin American Studies Assn			1				1
Middle East Studies Assn.				3			3
American Oriental Society				2		1	3
American Assn. for the Advancement of Slavic Studies					8		8
LIBRARY ASSOCIATIONS							
American Library Assn.	1	1		3	6	2	13
Library Assn. (British)	2	3					5
Library Assn. (China)		1					1
Indian Library Assn.						1	1

Other less common associational affiliations -- American Academy of Political and Social Sciences, American Historical Association, American Anthropological Association, Association of American Geographers, and Deutsche Afrika Gesellschaft -- are further evidence of this group's specialist interests.

*Only one respondent belongs neither to an "area" association nor a library association.

of improving my expertise as an area specialist per se, ALA is a waste of time. (Bibliographer)

Our area bibliographers feel that they get more out of national 'area' association meetings than the professional library association meetings. (Administrator)

Rank and Salary by Professional Experience as Bibliographer

It was assumed that the experience of the area bibliographer would be a determining factor in the expectations of library administrators and faculty towards the qualifications of bibliographers in building objective area collections. It was felt that if any area of book selection had been relegated to librarians it was to those area bibliographers who had had several years' experience. That the area bibliographers should be partially responsible for book selection in their area program was borne out in the data presented. What was surprising was that this expectation, expressed by 80 percent of the respondents, cut across experience lines; that is, this activity was expected of all bibliographers, no matter what their previous experience had been. There was no relationship expressed between the expectations of the respondents and the qualifications and experience of bibliographers working with area programs. The data presented in the following tables vary significantly; however, they do show some co-relationship between years of experience and salary. In this sense, they support earlier studies[20] which have maintained that salaries increase with professional experience. They do not, however, conform to Morrison's findings that length of experience is virtually unrelated to salary. [21]

People's interests often vary according to how many years' experience they have in a position; this is a general

proposition. In particular settings, such as university libraries, years of experience may have a variety of meanings
and be expressed in a number of ways. One of the ways
that bibliographers with more experience may claim special
consideration is through higher salaries and higher ranks,
if, indeed, rank is given. Tables 10-13 explore these possibilities.

Not infrequently, area bibliographers may hold joint
appointments in the library and in other departments of the
university. Twenty percent of the sample do hold such appointments. This type of appointment, emphasizing subject
specialization, probably makes the identification--which members of this group claim--with professions other than librarianship, even more legitimate. However, one faculty member cautions against joint appointments:

> Joint appointments with the library and with the
> area center are not necessary at all and make
> bibliographer's tenure highly insecure--as experi-
> ence here showed. (Language Professor)

The attitude of the area bibliographer toward being
considered faculty is reflected in responses to the question:
"Where, in the organization of the university, would you
place yourself?" Forty percent of the respondents consider
themselves faculty.

Some comments by faculty and library administrators
support the idea that the area bibliographer should have rank,
salary, and other privileges of the faculty:

> Where the bibliographer has full control, his edu-
> cational background must be as good as any faculty
> member's--and as broad. In any case, since he
> will be working closely with the faculty, it is es-
> sential that he have faculty rank even though he
> still is first and foremost a librarian. (Adminis-
> trator)

TABLE 10

SALARY BY NUMBER OF YEARS
EXPERIENCE AS A BIBLIOGRAPHER

SALARY RANGE	YEARS OF EXPERIENCE					
	1-3 n=7	4-6 n=7	7-9 n=7	10-12 n=5	13-15 n=2	Over 16* n=2
$8,600-$9,900	4	3	1	1		
$10,000-$11,400	3	1	1			
$11,500-$12,900		1	1	2		
$13,000-$14,400		2	2		1	
$14,500-$15,900			1	2		
$16,000-$17,900			1			
Over $18,000					1	

*Two respondents did not answer the salary question; both of them have had over 16 years experience.

TABLE 11

RANK BY NUMBER OF YEARS
EXPERIENCE AS A BIBLIOGRAPHER

RANK*	YEARS OF EXPERIENCE					
	1-3 n=7	4-6 n=7	7-9 n=7	10-12 n=5	13-15 n=2	Over 16 n=2
Professor				2		
Assoc. Prof.	1	1				
Asst. Prof.	1	3	1	2	1	
Instructor	3	1				1
Rank in Name Only		1	3	1		
No Rank	2	1	3	1		1

*Rank is given as faculty rank or equivalent -- the distinction is not made here, although it was made in the original data.

TABLE 12

CO-RELATIONSHIP OF EDUCATION WITH SALARY

SALARY*	Masters (or equivalent) in Library Science	Masters in subject (no Library Science)	Masters in subject plus masters in Library Science	2 masters in subject plus masters in Library Science	Doctorate plus masters in Library Science	Doctorate plus masters in subject (no Library Science)
				HIGHEST DEGREE EARNED		
$8,600-$9,900	4		5			
$10,000-$11,400	2		2	1		
$11,500-$12,900	1		2	1		
$13,000-$14,400	2	1	1		1	
$14,500-$15,900	1		1		1	
$16,000-$17,900						1
Over $18,000						1

*Salary not supplied by two (2) respondents.

TABLE 13

CO-RELATIONSHIP OF EDUCATION WITH RANK

RANK*	HIGHEST DEGREE EARNED					
	Masters (or equivalent) in Library Science	Masters in subject (no Library Science)	Masters in subject plus masters in Library Science	2 masters in subject plus masters in Library Science	Doctorate plus masters in Library Science	Doctorate plus masters in subject (no Library Science)
Professor				1		1
Associate Professor	1					1
Assistant Professor	1	1	6			
Instructor	2	1	2			
Rank in Name Only		5	5			
No Rank	1				1	1

*Rank is given as faculty rank or equivalent -- the distinction is not made here although it was made in the original data.

In general the area bibliographer must work closely
with the staff and faculty of the area program. He
or she should be accepted as a full member of the
area program. (Political Science Professor)

I would conceive of the office of the bibliographer
as essentially of a library nature, hence administrative rather than faculty. I would support the
notion that the office should enjoy all the benefits
of administrative offices which, in most cases,
seem to be equivalent to faculty benefits. (Art
Professor)

The bibliographer, although he should not have ten-
ure, should not be subject either to dismissal or
short notice. Library rank and salary should have
counter part to faculty rank. (Political Science
Professor)

A lot depends on the specialist's qualifications.
Professor [X] . . . was highly respected as a
scholar-librarian in the European sense--without a
library degree--and as a historian. I speculate
that Americans working for library degrees are
going to have more and more limited 'scholarly'
training. (Anthropology Professor)

Here at [X] . . . university, we fully recognize
the immense value rendered by special area librarians and bibliographers. I can only hope that we
implement this recognition suitably--i. e. , salary
and privileges. (Fine Arts Professor)

As a believer in full faculty rank and status for
professional academic librarians, I believe that
area bibliographers should be both faculty and librarians. (Bibliographer)

Despite these opinions, what was actually borne out in
the statistical data was that faculty members assume that
their colleagues are quite able to select materials for their
courses but they regard the librarian as needing help.   That
is, area bibliographers are not accorded true academic status
in the eyes of faculty, regardless of experience.   The opinion

that faculty assistance is necessary for building area collections was expressed in the following, which were typical faculty comments:

> I feel that in many, or even most cases, enough
> money is not available for the area specialist to
> effect the developments needed for the efficient
> functioning of the area collections. Given a first
> class area specialist bibliographer and sufficient
> support in funds and supporting staff, then and only
> then can efficient service be possible.   (Professor
> of Art)

> Area collections should be built with the advice and
> consent of the area faculty, never solely by the
> bibliographer.   (Anthropology Professor)

> It boils down to one major issue--is the area spe-
> cialist a faculty member virtually initiating research
> and determining library purchases or is he a li-
> brarian responsive in the functional sense to faculty
> needs? I go for the latter very strongly.   (English
> Professor)

> A bibliographer could be a faculty member or a
> librarian or both. If he is a librarian he must
> work closely with the faculty for they should, and
> do usually, determine the nature and scope of col-
> lections; nor are librarians, generally, competent
> to make such decisions and thus channel faculty and
> student research.   (Linguistics Professor)

> Area bibliographers are fortified alibis for not
> working.   Abolish all such titles and get on with
> the job of making material available.   (Economics
> Professor)

Place in the Library Organization

The area bibliographer's responsibilities overlap both
technical and public services aspects of traditional library
operations.   This is, perhaps, inherent in the development
of the area bibliographer position.   Most library support for

area programs began with a single employee in a technical
services department of the library, who served all aspects
necessary. Holding the area bibliographer responsible for
creating and servicing the special area collections, within
the main library, is still a fairly common practice. Only
23 percent of the area bibliographers in this sample are responsible for separate reading rooms or departmental libraries. Most of the remaining programs have the materials integrated with the general collection.

There do not appear to be special circumstances which
make a separate library necessary for one "area" collection
but not for another. Certainly Slavic and Latin American
collections, because of the alphabets, are the ones most
easily integrated into the general collection, yet two of the
separate collections which were reported were of Slavic materials. The bibliographer in a majority of the remaining
cases is located in technical services despite the fact that
most bibliographers, faculty, and administrators feel that he
should be in a public service area easily accessible to the
public.

To the statement: "Because of his responsibilities,
the area specialist bibliographer should be easily accessible
in a public area of the library," 58 percent responded in the
affirmative, 29 percent were neutral, and only 12 percent
disagreed. This evidence seems to support the contention
that the area bibliographer's responsibilities are not well defined and that confusion does exist as to his responsibilities
and place in the organization of the university library. The
confusion and disagreement on this point is reflected in some
comments:

> I think the area specialist bibliographer's most im-
> portant responsibilities are those related to building

the collection. Someone else can face the public. (History Professor)

The area specialist bibliographer should have an easily reached office, but not be in a reading area or at a reference desk. (Administrator)

Specialist bibliographers should be available to users for consultation, but only after regular public services consultants are unable to assist. (Political Science Professor)

Reasonable opportunity should be provided for privacy and concentrated working time without interruption, therefore he should be accessible to the public only part of the time. (Administrator)

The area bibliographer should be accessible to faculty in the area and to students who can use the materials in the languages of the area but the burden on the area bibliographer is usually so great that the bibliographer should be assured of space and privacy. This is particularly true of areas where the languages are usually not known by any but a few assistants to the area bibliographer and the area staff has to perform all the ordering, cataloging, and clerical functions. (Economics Professor)

They must be given major public service responsibility in the library as subject specialist consultants and reference staff with office hours and desk duties if necessary in the Reference Department and/ or in a portion of the open bookstack and reading area nearest 'their' part of the collection. They must be kept totally out of technical services, ordering, cataloging, etc. (Administrator)

Area bibliographers, despite their specialized interests, do have a good working knowledge of the colonial languages of their "area" and/or of the major languages within the "area," and accept responsibilities for the whole "area." They perform the role of true general area-wise specialists.

General expectations of area bibliographers were well

summarized in the following comment made by one library
administrator:

> I believe that the area specialist should be un-
> equivocally a librarian with a professional library
> education and academic competence in an appropri-
> ate subject field or fields. He needs the inde-
> pendence and professional expertise reflected in
> his library appointment combined with the academic
> and personal qualifications to assure acceptance
> and respect from faculty members. Nothing less
> will really fill the bill.

Summary

Analysis of the qualitative data, the non-scalable
portion of the descriptive profile of the area bibliographer,
revealed that the area bibliographer is a generalist in a special "area." His educational background, particularly his
knowledge of languages, qualifies him to handle the role of
a general area specialist, this being the responsibility he
has been assigned.

The statistical data and mechanical treatment of it,
because of format, have not been included in this revision
of the study. However, application of statistical tests to
responses of faculty and library administrators revealed no
dependencies, on the background variables of education, experience, and language knowledge, significant enough to support a statement that there is a relationship between the expectations of faculty and library administrators toward certain
qualifications important to the bibliographer role and actual
possession of those background variables by the bibliographer.
It must be remembered, however, that there are many factors other than attitudes and background variables which are
involved in roles and role playing. The strongest of these
is probably personality. This is one area of strain which

was not explored in this study but which must be mentioned
here. Personality characteristics of group members can
influence their expectations of others and that is one of the
most important elements which is used in the analysis of
role strain. This line of reasoning is embedded in theory
and finds supporting evidence in research. [22]

Another point which must be made here is that responses to the questionnaire were slanted to the right on
questions involving qualifications, indicating high expectations
by both faculty and library administrators. This, plus the
high qualifications which the area specialist bibliographers
exhibited, may have produced a skewness in the data. What
was not anticipated in the beginning of this study was that
such a large percentage of area bibliographers would be so
qualified.

Having thus analyzed some characteristics of the area
specialist bibliographer and his place in the complex university organization, the next chapter will attempt to determine
the expectations of certain groups of people toward the bibliographer's role and the perceptions of the bibliographers
themselves toward that role.

Notes

1.   See, for example: S. H. Osipow, Theories of Career
     Development (New York: Appleton-Century-Crofts,
     1968).

2.   This "control" group's background data was drawn from:
     A Biographical Directory of Librarians in the United
     States and Canada, ed. by Lee Ash (5th ed. ; Chicago:
     American Library Association, 1970); Who's Who in
     Library Service, ed. by Lee Ash (4th ed. ; Hamden,
     Conn. : Shoe String Press, 1966); and A Biographical
     Directory of Librarians in the Field of Slavic and
     East European Studies, comp. and ed. by Peter A.

Goy (Chicago: American Library Association, 1967).

3. Neal Gross and Anne E. Trask, Men and Women as Elementary School Principals, Final Report No. 2, Contract No. 853 (SAE-8702), U. S. Office of Education (Cambridge, Mass: Harvard Graduate School of Education, 1964), p. 1.

4. Edward Gross, Work and Society (New York: Thomas Y. Crowell, 1958), p. 158.

5. U. S. Women's Bureau, "Fact Sheet on Women in Professional and Technical Positions" (Washington, D. C. : Women's Bureau, November, 1966), p. 1.

6. Anita R. Schiller, Characteristics of Professional Personnel in College and University Libraries, Final Report, Project No. 5-0919-2-22-1, Contract No. OE-6-10-200 (Urbana, Ill. : Library Research Center, Graduate School of Library Science, Research Series No. 16, May, 1968), p. 20.

7. John F. Harvey, The Librarian's Career: A Study of Mobility, ACRL Microcard Series No. 85 (Rochester, N. Y. : University of Rochester Press for the Association of College and Research Libraries), p. 149.

8. Schiller, op. cit. , p. 36.

9. Robert R. Douglas, "The Personality of the Librarian" (unpublished Ph. D. dissertation, Graduate Library School, University of Chicago, 1957), p. 59.

10. See particularly Perry D. Morrison, The Career of the Academic Librarian; A Study of the Social Origins, Educational Attainments, Vocational Experience, and Personality Characteristics of a Group of American Academic Librarians (Chicago: American Library Association, 1969), pp. 19-20; and Louis R. Wilson, "The Objectives of the Graduate Library School in Extending the Frontiers of Librarianship, " in New Frontiers in Librarianship (Chicago: Graduate Library School, University of Chicago, 1940), p. 21.

11. David C. Weber, "The Place of 'Professional Specialists' on the University Library Staff, " College and Research Libraries, XXVI, No. 5 (September, 1965), 383.

12. Schiller, op. cit. , p. 30.

13. Morrison, op. cit. , pp. 24-25.

14. Schiller, op. cit. , p. 40.

15. J. Periam Danton, "Doctoral Study in Librarianship in the United States, " College and Research Libraries, XX, No. 6 (November, 1959), 449.

16. Frederick H. Wagman, "The General Research Library and the Area-Studies Program, " Library Quarterly, XXXV, No. 4 (October, 1965), 351.

17. Harvey, op. cit. , p. 128.

18. Morrison, op. cit. , p. 63.

19. Schiller, op. cit. , p. 20.

20. Ibid. , p. 86.

21. Morrison, op. cit. , pp. 57-58.

22. See Robert K. Merton and Alice S. Kitt, "Contributions to the Theory of Reference Group Behavior, " in Continuities in Social Research, ed. by Robert K. Merton and Paul F. Lazarsfeld (Glencoe, Ill. : The Free Press, 1950), pp. 40-105; and J. W. Getzels and E. G. Guba, "Role, Role Conflict, and Effectiveness: An Empirical Study. " American Sociological Review. XIX, No. 2 (April, 1954), 164-75.

Chapter IV

ROLE PERCEPTIONS AND EXPECTATIONS

Introduction

Many of the factors which determine the role of the area bibliographer relate to his responsibilities within the organization. The primary purpose of this chapter is to examine that role through the expectations of area faculty and library administrators and through the perceptions of the bibliographer himself. Baumgartel points out that there is a real source of difficulty about the disagreement which can arise concerning what functions a person in a particular role should perform.[1] Awareness of these disagreements should help the area bibliographer to structure his behavior to prevent future strain and to develop perceptions consistent with effective role performance. Other people's appreciations for his role might also be improved as a consensus is reached. Finally, the university library using or contemplating using area bibliographers will, hopefully, be able to arrive at a better job definition for the bibliographer.

Assumptions that the structural requirements for any professional position are defined with a high degree of explicitness, clarity, and consensus among all the parties involved have not been substantiated by research findings which express, rather, a failure of consensus regarding proper roles of professional people.[2] Therefore, in attempting to characterize or analyze role requirements, one must guard

against the assumption that they are unified and logically coherent.

Ackerman maintains that the extent to which a role
is successfully handled is a function of the degree of overlap between the role expectations and the doer's own needs.
The individual is most likely to handle best, from among
several roles, the one whose expectations are most nearly
congruent with his needs. [3] No matter what major role he
may select, he must face the realities of the situation in
which he finds himself.   He cannot long ignore the legitimate
expectations of others upon him without retaliation from them.
In this sense, an accepted progression of role elements is
expressed thus:

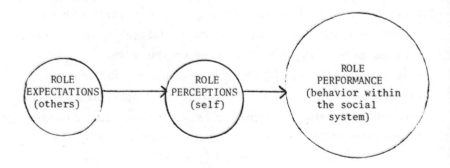

Figure 3. -- Elements of Role

> The way a person performs his role depends partly
> upon the expectations of others and partly upon his
> own perceptions of that role.   The clearer his per-
> ceptions and the stronger he is motivated, the more
> his behavior will agree with the expectations of
> others and the more they will agree with his per-
> formance. [4]

Some studies have shown that there is a strong relationship between a person's perception of his own role and

the expectations which he attributes to others. [5] Perceptions
and expectations are a part of the group themselves.   The
findings of this study should tell us about the extent to which
the bibliographer group has assimilated and taken on the
color of other groups and the extent to which they perceive
themselves as members of other groups.   It should also reveal the extent to which they have established their own territories and, in so doing, have achieved job satisfaction.

The attitudes of the academic groups toward the bibliographer's responsibilities have important implications for
the area programs in universities.   The efficiency with which
the bibliographer fulfills his obligations will be largely determined by the professional attitudes which he and others
bring to these responsibilities.   Attitudes toward his responsibilities are, therefore, significant aspects of his professional
status.

The Bibliographer's Role

What are the attitudes regarding activities theoretically
expected of the area specialist bibliographer?   Considered
in this section, in connection with the expectations and perceptions, are both the frequencies with which they were held
and the discrepancies among them.   The questionnaire included a group of items which were assumed to be associated
with the area bibliographer's responsibilities.   The identifi-
cation of these responsibilities and functions, for the purposes of this questionnaire, was by no means exhaustive, nor
was it intended to establish professional territories.   Rather,
this examination of role determinations was directed toward
the understanding of relationships in the organization.   It
should be pointed out that the range of responses on the atti-

tude portion of the questionnaire was from one through five
but, for conveniences in making comparisons, the responses
in the "Strongly Agree" and "Agree" categories were combined as were the ones in the "Disagree" and "Strongly Disagree" categories. Practices for which there was no statistical difference and which received by far the largest responses of four or five by each group were judged to display
role consensus as seen by the three groups of respondents.
Practices which revealed no statistical difference but for
which a large percentage of "Neutral" responses were indicated by each group were judged to be optional practices.
Whenever a practice varied greatly from a pre-established
statistical level it was judged to indicate a practice that did
not display role consensus. In those cases further analysis
between groups was made to determine the source of disagreement. It is within this lack of role consensus that
strain or dissatisfaction probably arises over the role of the
area specialist bibliographer.

        Tabulation procedures disclosed the extent to which
the role expectation/perception of the bibliographer was at
variance among the types of respondents. The analysis in
this chapter reflects four approaches: (1) role as perceived
by the bibliographer; (2) role as expected by library administrators; (3) role as expected by area faculty; and (4) con-
gruence of the role as expected/perceived by all respondents.
Again, it must be pointed out that the detailed statistical
portion of this study have been removed from this portion of
the study so that they would not distract from the easy flow
of the primary points being made.

Proximity Among the Three Groups

        All three groups were closely in agreement on several

of the activities described in the questionnaire.   Some conception of the degree of accord among the groups, concerning those "agreement" items, may be gleaned from an examination of the following items.   On four activities there
was a relatively high degree of consensus among expecta-
tions/perceptions of all three groups.   These items included:

1.   Discovers new publications in pertinent fields of
interest through systematic perusal of bibliographies, publishers' catalogs, and reviews in journals.   Ninety-seven percent of the respondents agree that this is a major activity
of the area bibliographer.

2.   Follows regularly and systematically comprehensive bibliographies and dealers' catalogs.   Only one respondent indicated that this is not a major activity of the
area bibliographer.

3.   Knows book trade and bibliographies of all countries within the "area. "   Ninety-six percent of the respondents agree that this is an important activity of the area bibliographer.

4.   Tries to secure all requests made by the faculty.
Again, only one respondent felt that the bibliographer should
not participate, completely, in this activity.   This was qualified by the statement that:

> Some faculty members are ignorant of what is
> available in their own areas, and what makes
> sense for a library's over-all growth.   And some
> desire total blanket, unevaluated, coverage of their
> research project.   The specialist should try to
> steer a sensible course--if he or she is senior
> enough to avoid having to do whatever the faculty
> asks.   (Anthropology Professor)

In addition to the overall agreement among the groups
as to those activities mentioned above, there was another

group of activities which showed no statistical difference in
the expectations/perceptions among the groups.   These activities appear in Table 14.   While the groups varied in their
responses to the specific responsibilities enumerated, their
responses tended, statistically, to reflect a reasonably high
degree of accord among the groups.   Four of these items
were so strongly in favor of the activity being described that
they should perhaps be added to the previous number on
which there seemed to be complete accord as to the desirability of the bibliographer participating in the described activity.   Eighty-eight percent of the respondents felt that the
bibliographer should work with faculty members in identifying
new areas of collection developments.   Emphasis should,
however, not be placed on working with each individual faculty
member.   As one economics professor points out:

> A faculty is made up of diverse individuals and as
> individuals they establish their own relationship
> with the area bibliographer, the research collection,
> the teaching collection and with the acquisitions
> process.

An administrator further maintained that:

> It is not necessary to work with each faculty mem-
> ber individually to identify new areas of responsi-
> bility for collection development.   This can be done
> with the aid of profile of interest charts, question-
> naires, or a faculty member who represents the
> 'area. '

Ninety percent of each group agreed that checking with
the faculty before going on buying trips is desirable, while
85 percent felt that the bibliographer should keep the faculty
and graduate students aware of new publications of interest
to them.   The typical respondent to this item expressed the
belief that:

TABLE 14

ACTIVITIES CONCERNING WHICH EXPECTATIONS/PERCEPTIONS DID NOT VARY SIGNIFICANTLY AMONG GROUPS*
(Combined Group Analysis)

ACTIVITY	d.f.	x^2
1. When going on buying trip, checks to see if the interests of faculty are being taken into consideration.	4	2.06
2. Works individually with each faculty member to identify new areas of responsibility for collection development.	4	4.96
3. Tries to keep the faculty and graduate students aware of new publications of interest to them.	4	6.02
4. Prepares bibliographies for faculty and student use.	4	7.09
5. Has knowledge of library techniques for which a library degree is desirable.	4	4.81
6. Constructs a desiderata file and continues to search for out-of-print materials in all languages concerned.	4	1.68
7. Supervises or advises on orders placed with all domestic and foreign book dealers specializing in the "area".	4	9.17
8. Attends national professional library association meetings.	4	6.27

*x^2 value with 4 degrees of freedom must be 9.48 or larger for the difference between expectations/perceptions to be significantly different at the .05 level.

> The key function is contacts with faculty and gradu-
> ate students to relate acquisition to current and
> future curriculum. (Political Science Professor)

The last activity on which there was a strong consensus was the necessity of constructing desiderata files and
searching for out-of-print materials. Eighty-eight percent
of the respondents felt that this was an important activity
for the bibliographer to perform. However, some bibliographers questioned the priority of this activity:

> The time spent in assembling a desiderata file is
> better spent in attacking dealers' catalogs while
> they are fresh, and in writing to dealers for three
> or four titles--books or periodical backfiles--at a
> time.

It was also pointed out that:

> The less experienced librarian or the librarian
> with less knowledge of the bibliography of his area
> may be forced to construct such a desiderata list
> as the only means he has of identifying significant
> titles lacking from the collection.

Four activities for which there was no statistical difference in opinions but for which there was no strong expression of need for the activity were also revealed in this
analysis. The first two of these deal directly with the field
of librarianship. About 40 percent of the respondents were
negative or neutral toward the desirability of area bibliographers attending national professional library association
meetings. As one history professor remarked:

> That the area specialist bibliographer must attend
> national professional library association meetings
> is unavoidable, but a waste.

Surprisingly, there also was no strong feeling on the need
for the bibliographer to possess a library degree. Over

one-fourth of the respondents thought that the degree was unnecessary. This, of course, has strong implications for the
profession. If library skills can be performed by non-librarians, where does this lead us in terms of professional
status? One art professor summed up his observations by
stating:

> One of our very good [area] librarians had no li-
> brary training but was excellent as a bibliographer
> and builder of the library.

Thirdly, in the actual placing of orders or supervising
the ordering, there was no strong feeling that this is an important activity of the area bibliographer--over one-fifth of
the respondents were negative or neutral about this practice.

Finally, there was no strong consensus that the area
bibliographer should actually prepare bibliographies and
guides for faculty and student use. Over one-half of the
respondents felt that this was not an activity for the bibliographer to participate in. As one administrator stated:

> Our bibliographers don't have time to prepare
> bibliographies.

It is evident that this activity is far down the line of prior-
ities in the bibliographer's work role.

Divergence of the Three Groups

Having thus revealed the items which did not show
significant differences among the three groups, the next step
was to examine those items for which there was a significant
difference in expectations/perceptions and to determine which
of the three groups of role definers contributed most conspicuously to that difference. In order to determine where
these differences lay, a between-group analysis was performed.

This analysis, plus comparison of each group's frequencies
of response, points to those groups which by their divergence
contributed most significantly to the differences.   This type
of investigation of the expectations /perceptions revealed both
similarities between groups and differences between them.
Twelve activities, on which there was disagreement between
groups as to the responsibilities of bibliographers in performing them, are presented in Table 15.

Faculty Divergence

        By their divergence, generally in the direction of less
agreement, faculty contributed most prominently to the differences associated with seven of these twelve activities.
The nature of the activities on which this difference occurred
suggests that incongruity in expectations /perceptions, between
the faculty on the one hand and the bibliographers and administrators on the other, is apt to be most conspicuous at
points where responsibilities between faculty and bibliographers overlap or at least are very closely related.

        The responsibility of weeding the collection was deemed
necessary by at least four-fifths of both the bibliographers
and the administrators, 80 percent and 88 percent respec-
tively.   However, 35 percent of the faculty felt that this was
a neutral or unnecessary practice.   Evidently faculty feel
that this is in the general area of their responsibility.   This
was expressed, however subtly, in the following comment by
a Professor of Area Studies:

> Concerning the subject of weeding, what seems
> 'useless' for some people might not be useless for
> others.   Often books, basically important for re-
> search, may have nothing to do with the curriculum.

TABLE 15

ACTIVITIES CONCERNING WHICH EXPECTATIONS/PERCEPTIONS
VARIED SIGNIFICANTLY AMONG GROUPS
(Combined Group Analysis)

ACTIVITY	d.f.	x^2	p.
1. Effectively weeds useless materials which might be received in bulk shipments such as those which might come from Latin America through LACAP or from other areas through PL480.	4	16.12	.01
2. Evaluates the effectiveness of the library collections as to how they relate to the curriculum.	4	26.06	.001
3. Visits that "area" of the world either for purposes of research or on buying trips.	4	10.94	.05
4. Participates in departmental or interdepartmental meetings concerned with area studies to represent the library.	4	24.95	.001
5. Keeps in touch with faculty and the library administration about problems in the development of area collections of concern to them.	4	12.73	.02
6. Performs advanced reference service.	4	15.52	.01
7. Instructs in library use to students in the area program.	4	11.96	.02
8. Coordinates book selection practices in the "area".	4	18.68	.001
9. Conducts exchange negotiations with universities and other agencies in "area" countries.	4	23.34	.001
10. Maintains close liaison with the area faculty and administration of area programs.	4	12.42	.02
11. Attends national "area" association meetings.	4	13.19	.02
12. Has responsibility for selection of all "area" materials.	4	46.08	.001

The faculty also was not as strongly committed to
the bibliographer's evaluating the collection in relationship
to the curriculum. The majority of administrators, 92 percent, and bibliographers, 89 percent, felt that this was a
desirable practice of the area bibliographer; only 62 percent
of the faculty agreed.

Both the bibliographers, 93 percent, and administrators, 97 percent, maintained that the area bibliographer
should participate in "area" faculty meetings to represent
the library. One bibliographer commented:

> The area specialist bibliographer should participate
> in departmental and interdepartmental meetings not
> merely to represent the library but to represent
> the discipline of bibliography. Such participation
> is actually the best method available to the librar-
> ian for keeping abreast of new developments, cur-
> riculum changes, changing research emphasis, etc.,
> within his area studies center or program.

The faculty did not feel nearly as strongly about this activity.
In fact, almost one-third felt, at best, that it is a neutral
activity for the bibliographer to perform. Perhaps this attitude of the bibliographer was a carry-over, as has been
indicated before, of the strong feeling that he is primarily
faculty, and the attitude of the faculty, on the other hand,
that he is not a qualified colleague and therefore has no
place in faculty meetings.

That none of the three groups expressed strong conviction that the bibliographer should keep in touch with faculty
and library administrators concerning problems in the development of area collections was not surprising. All three
groups, evidently, felt that this was something for the area
bibliographer to work out himself. The faculty, with almost
10 percent negative response and one-third neutral response,

contributed most to the variance in groups. Both bibliographers and administrators indicated, through the 25 percent neutral response from each group, that this was a questionable practice.

On the question of the necessity of the bibliographer to perform advanced reference service, there was no strong indication from any of the three groups that this was an absolutely necessary activity. On the contrary, a large percentage of all three groups indicated that this was a neutral practice. However, the faculty, with their 13 percent negative response, contributed most significantly to the difference. An indication of this neutral feeling was expressed by the following observations:

> I do not provide advanced reference service, and I am not certain that I would like to do so in the future though I recognize that in some libraries it might be desirable for a bibliographer to do so. I see my principal assignment as collection development. (Bibliographer)

> Bibliographers should be primarily in charge of getting books, not providing general reference service. (History Professor)

Another area in which there was basic disagreement between the faculty group and the bibliographer-administrator groups was that of coordinating book selection practices in the "area." The influence of the tradition of this activity being performed by faculty was most pronounced in faculty responses to this item. In the history of book selection, the activity has rested in the hands of faculty.

> It may be said that although the responsibility (for book selection in academic libraries in the United States) administratively and legally may, and frequently does reside in the library, it has generally been taken over, as a practical matter, by the fac-

> ulty. . . . The actual selection of books is largely
> carried out . . . by faculty members. [6]

Today there are some who believe that this has become a
joint effort between librarians and faculty. However, responses to this question indicate that almost one-third of the
faculty still felt that this was not a responsibility of the bibliographer but rather a prerogative of the faculty, while over
90 percent of both the administrative group and the bibliographer group felt that it was the bibliographer's responsibility:

> I believe the area specialist should do the work of
> book selection in his area--not just coordinate--
> consulting faculty and students occasionally when he
> feels the need for special advice. (Bibliographer)

This source of stress between librarians and faculty could
easily result in poor relations which nearly always surface
through some channel:

> A poor relationship between the library and the
> area faculty, which nearly always means between
> the bibliographer and the center, will inevitably
> reflect itself in faculty comment, usually unofficial
> but rarely unimportant. (Administrator)

The greatest disagreement seemed to appear in connection
with a related question concerning the responsibilities for
book selection. Over 50 percent of the faculty maintained
that this, at most, was a neutral practice of the area bibliographer, and 11 percent reported that, in their judgment,
it was not his responsibility but rather theirs. At the same
time, at least 90 percent of both the bibliographer and administrator groups responded that this was a necessary responsibility of the area bibliographer. As one administrator
pointed out:

> Coming as it has, at a time when many libraries
> were already making serious attempts to take a
> more active role in book selection, the concept of
> the area bibliographer has played a major role in
> shaping the form of that selection effort.

Evidently this selection responsibility is not as well estab-

lished as many would desire or even suppose:

> The bibliographer should have responsibility for
> selection of materials only in accordance with poli-
> cies established by area faculty committees. The
> committee should be able to overrule him, although
> he bears full responsibility for carrying out their
> policies. (Political Science Professor)

Bibliographer Divergence:

Bibliographers, by their divergence in the direction

of positive reaction toward the desirability of some responsi-

bilities, contributed most significantly to differences associ-

ated with three activities.

Most bibliographers, 93 percent, felt that it was de-

sirable for the area bibliographer to make buying trips to

his "area" of the world. At the same time, both adminis-

trators and faculty reacted neutrally to this activity. About

one-third of each of those groups felt it was unnecessary.

This was unexpected in view of the number of bibliographers,

particularly in African, South and Southeast Asian, and Far

Eastern programs, who had actually participated in such

ventures. It is possible that faculty and administrators in

certain programs--Slavic and Latin American being most

prominent areas where it is no longer absolutely necessary

to visit to acquire pertinent materials, these being the areas

which have developed some type of national bibliography and

standard book trade channels--could have accounted for a

large percentage of this disagreement.

Neither faculty nor administrators reacted strongly to
the desirability of the bibliographer instructing students in
library use. Over one-fourth of each of these groups said
that this activity was a neutral practice, while almost 10 percent of each of those groups indicated that it was an undesirable undertaking. At the same time, 97 percent of the bibliographers perceived this as part of their work role. This
was qualified by the comment of one bibliographer:

> My role, in instructing students, would be only to
> supplement the orientation programs with an intro-
> duction to bibliographies in the 'area. '

Likewise, bibliographers varied from the other two
groups in their reactions to the necessity of attending national "area" association meetings. Ninety-six percent felt
it was probably a necessary part of their position. However,
both faculty and administrators generally disagreed. Two-
thirds of the faculty and 80 percent of the administrators
reasoned that this was not a part of the bibliographer's role.
Again, perhaps this strong reaction, on the part of bibliographers, could be related to their desire of relating to faculty in the area program.

Administrator Divergence:

Administrators, through their strong neutral reaction
to one item and their strong positive reaction to another,
contributed most significantly to the difference between groups
on the remaining two items.

It was revealed that, although none of the three groups
reacted strongly in favor of the bibliographer conducting exchange negotiations with "area" sources, the administrators,
by their overwhelming neutrality, were most conspicuous in

their differences. Evidently there was some agreement that the bibliographer should act only as a consultant in such negotiations. As one bibliographer indicated:

> On the point of exchange negotiations, decisions as to which libraries to exchange with should be made in consultation with the bibliographer who in his travels has presumably had a first-hand view of the libraries and the materials available for exchange.

Finally, the administrators expressed stronger support for the necessity of the bibliographer maintaining close liaison with the "area" faculty and administration than did the other two groups. Only about one-fourth of the administrators felt this was a neutral practice while almost 50 percent of both other groups expressed the opinion that this was a truly neutral practice, that it was probably not desirable for the bibliographer to concern himself with such activities. However, one administrator qualified his support by stating:

> It is obvious that close liaison with the money source, be it library or an 'area' program budget, is absolutely necessary.

Summary

These findings should have implications for developing "area" programs in academic communities as well as for recruiting personnel. Item analysis of each group's frequencies of response pointed to those groups which by their divergence contributed most conspicuously to the between group differences.

Conspicuous among the findings is the large proportion of "agreement" activities which are theoretically descriptive of the bibliographer's role. Eight activities were identified as having role consensus. These were descriptive of prac-

tices that area specialist bibliographers, library administrators, and area faculty all felt were desirable functions for
the bibliographer. All eight of these activities were deemed
necessary by at least 85 percent of the respondents. These
included, in order of their percentage of agreement:

1. Following systematically comprehensive bibliographies and dealers' catalogs. (99%)

2. Trying to secure all requests by the faculty. (99%)

3. Discovering new materials in pertinent fields through
   systematic perusal of bibliographies, publishers'
   catalogs and reviews in journals. (97%)

4. Knowing the book trade and bibliographies of all
   countries within the "area." (96%)

5. When going on buying trips, checking to make sure
   the interests of the faculty are taken into consideration. (91%)

6. Working with faculty to identify new areas for collection development. (88%)

7. Constructing desiderata files and searching for out-
   of-print materials in all languages. (88%)

8. Keeping the faculty and graduate students aware of
   new publications of interest to them. (85%)

The largest share of agreements in expectations/perceptions,
then, relates specifically to those "bibliographic" operations
which might rightfully be expected of all bibliographers,
whether area, subject, or general.

Eight practices were identified as exhibiting some
role strains, an interpretation based on the lack of role consensus among the three groups concerning those activities.
Positive expectations/perceptions for those activities tended
to be highest among the bibliographers themselves, lowest
among faculty, with administrators providing the balancing

force.   Administrators' views of the area bibliographer's
role were more similar to the views of the area bibliographer than were the faculty's.   This suggests that there is
greater potential for dissatisfaction or strain between the
area bibliographer and the faculty than between the administrator and the bibliographer or between the administrator and
the faculty member.   This seems to indicate that the administrator's view of the role of the area specialist bibliographer reflects the majority of opinions of the other two
groups.   In addition to the overall differences among groups,
there was a low consensus between groups with regard to
these activities.   The most sensitive areas are those in
which the faculty disagreed with the bibliographer-administrator groups.   These five items reflect the traditional approach to collection development which is still evident in the
faculty's differences.   A large percentage of faculty disagreed
with the involvement of area bibliographers in the following
activities.   Items are ranked in order of disagreement, per-
centagewise, by the faculty:

1. Book selection responsibilities.   (50%)

2. Evaluating the collections in relation to the curriculum.   (37%)

3. Weeding materials from area collections.   (35%)

4. Coordinating book selection practices.   (29%)

5. Participating in faculty meetings.   (28%)

Despite what might be expected--that area bibliographers
would be assimilated into the book selection activities and
thus be expected to perform those functions--this was not
entirely borne out in the expectations as expressed by the
faculty in this sample.   By far the largest share of strain

between groups related to those activities.

The other area of divergence between groups was between the bibliographer and the faculty-administrator groups.
The bibliographer's divergence was in the opposite direction
from that noted above by the faculty.   The bibliographer
group reacted more positively to certain activities they
deemed desirable:

1. Attending national "area" association meetings.
   (96%)

2. Instructing students in library use of "area" materials.   (96%)

3. Participating in buying trips to that "area" of the
   world.   (93%)

No pattern could be discerned to account for the variations
of bibliographers from the other groups on these particular
activities.

Finally, several optional activities, contingent upon
the desire of the persons concerned, were also identified.
Among those which were described, at best, neutral by all
respondents were, in order of neutrality:

1. Preparing bibliographies for faculty and student
   use.   (42%)

2. Maintaining close liaison with "area" faculty and
   administration.   (41%)

3. Attending national professional library association
   meetings.   (39%)

4. Keeping in touch with faculty and library administrators about problems in the area collection.   (34%)

5. Performing advanced reference service.   (31%)

6. Conducting exchange negotiations.   (26%)

   7. Possessing knowledge of library techniques.   (26%)

   8. Supervising orders placed for "area" materials.
       (21%)

All of these activities could be considered peripheral and not
specifically tied to basic work roles for area bibliographers.
Interestingly, it is in this group of activities where the
greatest divergence from what might be expected as "necessary" was found. Things like maintaining close liaison with
the faculty, preparing bibliographies and performing reference
service, and even knowledge of library techniques for which
a library degree is desirable, all would seem to be important aspects of the bibliographer's role.   Group attitudes in
this study did not support those assumptions.

       These conclusions would suggest that the area bibli-
ographer does not always fully meet expectations that others
have of his role.   There is some confusion among role-de-
fining groups as to what is the bibliographer's appropriate
role.   One general proposition is that the more complex an
occupation becomes and the more roles a person is required
to perform in order to fulfill occupational expectations, the
more likely he is to be exposed to these role strains.   Evidently the area bibliographer's role has reached that stage
of development.

       A diagrammatic representation of the divergences of
the bibliographer's functions is presented in Figure 4.

       In summary, two comments from administrators seem
appropriate here:

> Presumably he should possess what you might call
> book sense by which he can distinguish chat from
> research and relate his selection to some purpose
> other than the aggrandizement of the collections.
> He should be all the things specified in the ques-
> tionnaire and even though he fails invariably to be

Figure 4. Role Model of Area Bibliographer

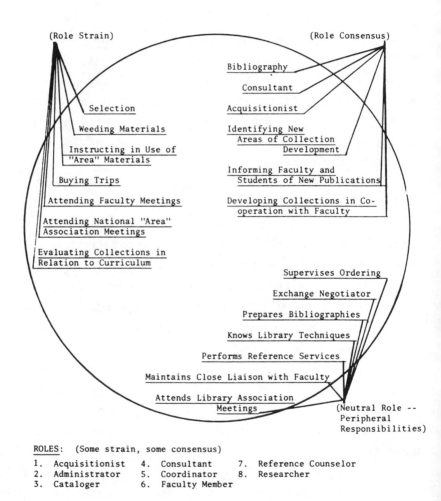

(Role Strain)   (Role Consensus)

Bibliography

Consultant

Selection   Acquisitionist

Weeding Materials   Identifying New
                             Areas of Collection
Instructing in Use of   Development
"Area" Materials
                             Informing Faculty and
Buying Trips   Students of New Publications

Attending Faculty Meetings   Developing Collections in Co-
                                  operation with Faculty
Attending National "Area"
Association Meetings

Evaluating Collections in
Relation to Curriculum

                                   Supervises Ordering

                                Exchange Negotiator

                             Prepares Bibliographies

                          Knows Library Techniques

                        Performs Reference Services

                  Maintains Close Liaison with Faculty

                   Attends Library Association
                              Meetings   (Neutral Role --
                                                  Peripheral
                                                  Responsibilities)

ROLES: (Some strain, some consensus)

1. Acquisitionist   4. Consultant   7. Reference Counselor
2. Administrator   5. Coordinator   8. Researcher
3. Cataloger   6. Faculty Member

this paragon of paragons he will not be wholly un-
effective if (1) he works at his job and in working
learns something about the collections already as-
sembled on the day he arrived; and (2) if he is
well informed, widely read, and eloquent, he can
be an asset to the organization.

The most important requirements, in my opinion,
are: (1) temperamental ability to work closely
with both faculty and library staff as a colleague,
and to adapt to the personal factors and organizational features of the library and the university;
(2) scholarly training and interests, though active
research seems to me less important, except as a
prestige factor. . . . I believe professional library
training to be of minor importance; (3) wide language competence appropriate to the field of responsibility; (4) a highly organized and systematic
mind, able to keep a complex operation going
steadily and productively. However, I think the
specialist should have his administrative responsibilities reduced as far as possible, though he must
of course manage his own staff; (5) personal factors
enabling him to work happily in a job frequently
frustrating and difficult -- optimism, a sense of
humor, interest in the problems of students and
faculty, etc. These are all essential.

Notes

1.   Howard Baumgartel, "The Concept of Role," in The
     Planning of Change, ed. by Warren G. Bennis,
     Kenneth D. Benne, and Robert Chin (New York: Holt,
     Rinehart and Winston, 1964), Part II, p. 374.

2.   See: J. Burling, Edith Lentz, and R. N. Wilson, The
     Give and Take in Hospitals (New York: Putnam,
     1956); N. Gross, W. S. Mason, and A. W. McEachern,
     Explorations in Role Analysis (New York: Wiley,
     1966); and A. Kornhauser, R. Dubin, and A. M. Ross,
     Industrial Conflict (New York: McGraw-Hill, 1954).

3.   Nathan W. Ackerman, "Social Role and Total Personal-
     ity," American Journal of Orthopsychiatry, XXI (Jan-
     uary, 1951), 1-17.

4. Hubert Bonner, Group Dynamics (New York: Ronald
    Press, 1959), p. 382.

5. Eugene Jacobson, W. W. Charters, Jr. , and Seymour
    Lieberman, "The Use of Role Concept in the Study
    of Complex Organizations, " Journal of Social Issues,
    VII, No. 3 (1951), 18-27.

6. J. Periam Danton, Book Selection and Collection, A
    Comparison of German and American University Li-
    braries (New York: Columbia University Press,
    1963), p. 34.

Chapter V

CONCLUSIONS AND RECOMMENDATIONS

Conclusions

The intent of this study was to describe the role and functions of the area specialist bibliographer as it was perceived by him and to describe the role as it was seen through the expectations of the faculty and library administration. It was designed to provide basic information regarding the bibliographer's work and to discover and describe areas of strain, as well as areas of consensus, in this role framework.

The data gathered in this study appear to warrant several conclusions. First, it is very clear that the area specialist bibliographer is a generalist in a profession where his educational background and experience qualify him for special responsibilities in the university library structure. His perception of himself as a generalist is largely due to the fact that he is involved in so many activities that often he isn't sure what he is or what he is not supposed to be.

Secondly, there is no significant relationship between the education, experience, and language knowledge of area specialist bibliographers and the expectations of faculty and library administrators toward those variables--at least in the population studies.

Finally, there exists among the bibliographer-faculty-administrator groups a general agreement on the desirable

113

practices of certain defined areas within the bibliographer's
role. However, there also exist within the bibliographer-
faculty-administrator interaction a substantial number of
practices which may cause role strain within the organization. It is toward those areas of role strain that the following recommendations are directed.

Recommendations

It may be assumed from the data presented in this
study that the role of the area bibliographer will continue to
be a nebulous one and one of some role strain until they
themselves do something about it. "A basic responsibility
of any professional is to redirect people's attitudes toward
his role and to cultivate public understanding and support."[1]
In this vein, should not the bibliographer's role be one of
specialization, not diversification; a role of uniqueness, not
generality? The bibliographer must articulate his own identity. Comparisons of data on what bibliographers perceive
as their responsibilities and what faculty and library administrators expect those responsibilities to be, revealed that
there is much disagreement on what they should and should
not do. They must communicate their role perceptions to
their public. Stronger communication with the faculty and
library administration, with the bibliographer acting as a
liaison agent, is recommended. If this is effectively done,
less strain is likely to arise. The area bibliographer, to
carry out this mission effectively, should be considered part
of the faculty of the area program; he should meet regularly
with the body and should be empowered to represent the library. He should specifically represent the discipline of
bibliography.

If the bibliographer's primary role is bibliography, then programs must be geared toward developing a person who possesses the skill and personal attributes that will enable him to feel comfortable and be effective in the job. Wide publicity of the need for specialization in academic libraries is urgently needed. Cooperative arrangements in universities that have accredited library schools and active area programs would, of course, be a first step in supplying the demand that exists for specialists in area programs. A few schools do have summer programs or workshops for practicing librarians and a couple do offer cooperative programs, but more are needed. Library schools should be encouraged to accept more cognate courses in area programs and should be encouraged to recognize the more "exotic" languages in addition to the standard western languages, French, German, Russian, and Spanish, which are now recognized by most library schools.

Libraries, too, should begin to recognize the importance of area bibliographers. They must realize the need for expertise in "areas." Hopefully, if this is done, specialists will no longer feel it necessary to go the "administrative" route to find recognition. Morrison found that "even though there may have been need for subject specialists with the doctorate in other types of library positions, the salaries and prestige of the top administrative posts won almost all of the candidates. "[2] Library administrators should re-evaluate the organization which encourages such moves, particularly in light of specialization and its importance in academic libraries.

The bibliographer and the faculty, it is clear, must continue to coordinate their efforts of book selection but the major responsibility, if there is to be a balanced, objective collection, should rest with the one full time specialist--the experienced area bibliographer. The area program, too, should make every effort to use the full potentialities of the bibliographer as a resource person.

Finally, the library administration and the area faculty, whether working with an established program or a completely new one, must make serious attempts to reach an understanding as to the role of the area bibliographer in the university; an understanding which would remove the role strain which has been revealed by this study.

Suggestions for Further Research

The implications for further research that this study reveals are suggested in the following comments.

No comprehensive study of the library problems with "area" materials has yet been done. The Nunn-Tsien and Ruggles-Mostecky studies come near, but they are now out of date. There is a need for some well-based guides available to planners of area collections. Studies similar to those mentioned above should be conducted for other areas, and those studies which have been cited should be brought up to date to give us an idea of the comprehensiveness of our "area" coverages.

A comprehensive case study of a given library's problems with publications from all areas of the world would, perhaps, be another important approach.

Scientific evaluation of the research value of significant acquisitions plans--LACAP, PL 480, NPAC, etc.--is badly needed. Are these programs actually fulfilling their roles?

All the principal problems involved in selection, acquisition and particularly cataloging, as well as reference, interlibrary loan, and interlibrary cooperation in building "area" collections are other important areas to be explored. The influence of the aforementioned mass buying and federal programs on activities of library personnel--bibliographers and catalogers--would be another important step in evaluating the influence of area collections on academic libraries, as would a historical analysis of the contributions of federal agencies and private corporations to area studies development in academic libraries.

Many other peripheral topics, such as the deterioration of paper, which is particularly noticeable in materials from some areas; difficulties of acquiring out-of-print materials from those "areas"; and evaluation of microfilm projects for "area" materials, are also important problems to be examined.

Notes

1. Joseph C. Bently, ed. , The Counselor's Role (Boston: Houghton-Mifflin Co. , 1968), p. 135.

2. Perry D. Morrison, The Career of the Academic Librarian; A Study of the Social Origins, Educational Attainments, Vocational Experience, and Personality Characteristics of a Group of American Academic Librarians (Chicago: American Library Association, 1969), p. 26.

Chapter VI

SELECTED BIBLIOGRAPHY

"Area" Sources Consulted

"Acquisition of Library Materials from Newly-Developing
    Areas of the World. " Library Resources and Tech-
    cal Services, VII, No. 3 (Winter, 1963), 1-46.

"African Studies in the United States. " African Studies Bul-
    letin, V (May, 1961), 9-19; VI (March, 1962), 19-28.

American Council on Education. "Inventory of NDEA Title
    VI: Language and Area Centers. " 1961. (Mimeo-
    graphed.)

Anderson, C. Arnold. "Comparative Education: Recom-
    mendations for Implementation of the International
    Education Act. " Prepared for the Assistant Secretary
    of Education, June, 1967. (Mimeographed.)

"Area Studies. " International Social Science Bulletin, IV
    (1952), 633-99.

Association for Asian Studies, Inc. Committee on East Asian
    Libraries. Library Resources on East Asia. Zug,
    Switzerland: Inter Documentation Co. , 1968.

Association of Research Libraries. "Report of the Joint
    Committee on African Resources, July-December,
    1963. " [Evanston, Ill. , 1964]. (Mimeographed.)

_____. Committee on National Needs. Working
    Paper, Section G. "Interim Report on the Adequacy
    of American Research Library Collections and Service
    Pertaining to Southeast Asia and the Far East. " [As-
    sociation of Research Libraries, October 20-22, 1951].
    (Multigraphed.)

Axelrod, Joseph. NDEA Language and Area Centers. Wash-
     ington, D. C. : U. S. Office of Education, 1964.

_____, and Bigelow, Donald N. Resources for Lan-
     guage and Area Studies: A Report on an Inventory
     of the Language and Area Centers Supported by the
     National Defense Education Act of 1958. Washington,
     D. C. : American Council on Education, 1962.

Barry, Paul L. "Development of Library Resources. " The
     Non-Western World in Higher Education. Edited by
     Donald N. Bigelow and Lyman H. Legters. Phila-
     delphia: American Academy of Political and Social
     Science, 1964.

Beal, Edwin G. , Jr. "East Asian Collections in America:
     Discussion. " Library Quarterly, XXXV, No. 4
     (October, 1965), 276-82.

Beckman, George M. "The Role of the Foundation. " The
     Non-Western World in Higher Education. Edited by
     Donald N. Bigelow and Lyman H. Legters. Phila-
     delphia: American Academy of Political and Social
     Science, 1964.

Benewick, Anne. "American Library and Area Studies. "
     Library Association Record, LXX (May, 1968), 117-19.

Bennett, Wendell C. Area Studies in American Universities.
     New York: Social Science Research Council, 1951.

_____. The Ethnographic Board. Smithsonian Mis-
     cellaneous Collection, No. 3899. Washington, D. C. :
     Smithsonian Institution, 1947.

Bigelow, Donald N. "A Backdoor to the Future. " Report
     of the Fourteenth Annual Round Table Meeting on
     Linguistics and Language Studies. Washington, D. C. :
     Georgetown University Press, 1963, pp. 156-66.

_____. "The Center Concept in Language and Area
     Studies. " The Linguistic Reporter, III (October,
     1961), 1-3.

_____, and Legters, Lyman H. NDEA Language and
     Area Centers; A Report on the First Five Years.
     Washington, D. C. : Government Printing Office, 1964.

_____, and Legters, Lyman H. , eds. "The Non-
Western World in Higher Education. " Annals of the
American Academy of Political and Social Science,
CCCLVI (November, 1964), i-141.

Boardman, Eugene P. , ed.   Asian Studies in Liberal Education; The Teaching of Asian History and Civilizations
to Undergraduates. Washington, D. C. :   Association
of American Colleges, 1959.

Bordie, John G. , ed.   National Conference on the Teaching
of African Languages and Area Studies.   Washington,
D. C. :   Georgetown University, 1960.

Borton, Hugh. "Asian Studies and the American Colleges. "
Journal of Asian Studies, XVIII (November, 1958),
59-65.

Brown, W. Norman, ed.   Resources for South Asian Language Studies in the United States.   Philadelphia:
University of Pennsylvania Press, 1960.

Buist, Eleanor.   "Area Programs for the Soviet Union and
East Europe - Some Current Concerns of the Libraries. " Library Quarterly, XXXV, No. 4 (October,
1965), 310-25.

_____. "Bibliographic and Research Aids in Soviet
Studies. " College and Research Libraries, XXVIII,
No. 5 (September, 1967), 317-25.

Byrnes, Robert F. "Area Programs for the Soviet Union
and East Europe - Some Current Concerns of the Libraries: Discussion. " Library Quarterly, XXXV,
No. 4 (October, 1965), 326-29.

_____, ed.   The Non-Western Areas in Undergraduate
Education in Indiana. Bloomington, Ind. :   Indiana
University Publications, 1959.

_____. "Reflections on American Training Programs
on Russia. " Slavic Review, XXI (September, 1962),
487-99.

_____. "Russian Studies: The Next Assignment. "
[May 15, 1967]. (Mimeographed.)

Cline, Howard F. , ed. Latin American Studies in the United
    States. Washington, D. C. : Library of Congress,
    1959.

Commission on International Understanding. Non-Western
    Studies in the Liberal Arts College; A Report. Wash-
    ington, D. C. : Association of American Colleges,
    1964.

Committee on the University and World Affairs. The Uni-
    versity and World Affairs. New York: Ford Founda-
    tion, 1960.

"Conference on American Library Resources on Southern
    Asia, November 19-22, 1957. " Journal of the Baroda
    (City) Oriental Institute, VIII (1959).

Creel, H. G. , ed. Chinese Civilization in Liberal Education.
    Chicago: University of Chicago Press, 1959.

Dean, Vera. The American Student and the Non-Western
    World. Cambridge, Mass. : Harvard University
    Press, 1956.

Dearnely, Carolyn, and Bixler, Paul H. "Latin American
    Collections. " Wilson Library Bulletin, XL (Decem-
    ber, 1967), 417-21.

Dudley, Norman. "A Library Administrator Views Area
    Study Collections. " Twelfth Seminar on the Acquisi-
    tion of Latin American Library Materials, Working
    Paper No. 4. [Washington, D. C. : Pan American
    Union, 1968], 167-73.

Duigan, Peter J. , ed. Handbook of Resources for African
    Studies. Stanford, Calif. : Hoover Institute, 1965.

Echols, John M. "The Southeast Asia Program and the Li-
    brary. " Library Quarterly, XXXV, No. 4 (October,
    1965), 239-53.

Ethnographic Board, Washington, D. C. Reports on Area
    Studies in American Universities. Washington, D. C. :
    Ethnographic Board, 1945.

Ettlinger, J. R. T. "Through a Glass Darkly. " APLA Bul-
    letin, (June, 1968), 32-40.

122   The Area Specialist Bibliographer

Fairbank, John King.   "A Note of Ambiguity: Asian Studies
    in America. "   Journal of Asian Studies, XIX (Novem-
    ber, 1959), 3-9.

Fenton, William Nelson.   Area Studies in American Univer-
    sities; For the Commission on Implications of Armed
    Services Educational Programs.   Washington, D. C. :
    American Council on Education, 1947.

Fife, Austin E. , and Nielsen, Marion L. , directors.   Re-
    port of the Conference on Neglected Languages,
    March 27-28, 1961.   New York: Modern Language
    Association of America, 1961.

Fisher, Harold H.   "Growing Pains of Slavic and East Euro-
    pean Area Training. "   American Slavic and East
    European Review, XVIII (October, 1958), 346-50.

Flapan, Maxwell.   "The World We Have to Know. "   Ameri-
    can Education, I, No. 8 (October, 1965), 30-32.

Flores, Edmundo.   "Latin American Studies: Library Needs
    and Problems: Discussion. "   Library Quarterly,
    XXXV, No. 4 (October, 1965), 340-42.

Forde, Darryl.   "Tropical African Studies. "   Africa, XXVX
    (January, 1965), 84-88. 92.

Foreign Area Research; A Conference Report.   [Washington,
    D. C.] Division of Behavioral Sciences, National
    Academy of Science, National Research Council, 1967.

Freeman, Stephen A.   "International Study at Home and
    Abroad. "   The Non-Western World in Higher Educa-
    tion.   Edited by Donald N. Bigelow and Lyman H.
    Legters.   Philadelphia: American Academy of Politi-
    cal and Social Science, 1964.

Fussler, Herman H.   "The General Research Library and
    the Area-Studies Programs: Discussion. "   Library
    Quarterly, XXXV, No. 4 (October, 1965), 355-60.

Georgetown University, Washington, D. C.   School of Foreign
    Service.   Institute of Language and Linguistics.
    Monograph Series on Area Studies, No. 1 - (April,
    1952-   )

Gibb, Sir Hamilton A. R. Area Studies Reconsidered. London: University of London, School of Oriental and African Studies, 1963.

Goy, Peter A. Russian Area Studies at the City College Library. [New York]: City University of New York, City College Library, 1964.

Graves, Mortimer. The Library of Congress PL-480 Foreign Acquisitions Program: User's View. New York: American Council of Learned Societies, 1969.

Great Britain. University Grants Committee. Report of the Sub-Committee on Oriental, Slavonic, East European and African Studies. London: H. M. Stationary Office, 1961.

Gumperg, Ellen M. Foreign Area Studies in American Higher Education. Berkeley, Calif. : University of California, Center for Research and Development in Higher Education, 1966.

Hadi, Muhammad Muhammad El-. "Arabic Library Resources in the United States: An Investigation of their Evolution, Status, and Technical Problems. " Unpublished Ph. D. dissertation, Graduate School of Library Science, University of Illinois, 1964.

Hall, Robert B. "Area Studies: With Special Reference to their Implications for Research in the Social Sciences. " Social Science Research Council Pamphlet No. 3. New York: Social Science Research Council, 1947.

Hallo, William W. "The Place of Oriental Studies in a University Curriculum. " Journal of Higher Education, XXVII (January, 1956), 11-17.

Harris, Chauncy D. "Area Studies and Library Resources. " Library Quarterly, XXXV, No. 4 (October, 1965), 205-17.

Harrison, John P. "Latin American Studies: Library Needs and Problems. " Library Quarterly, XXXV, No. 4 (October, 1965), 330-39.

Heindel, Richard Heathcote. The Present Position of Foreign Area Studies in the United States; A Post-Con-

ference Report. New York: Social Science Research
Council, Committee on World Area Research, 1950.

Hirsch, F. E.   "College Libraries and International Understanding. "   College and Research Libraries, VII
(April, 1946), 138-44.

Hotimsky, C. M.   "Slavic Studies and Libraries. "   Canadian
Library Journal, XXVII, No. 2 (March-April, 1970),
119-23.

Huang, C.   "Building an East Asian Library. "   Rochester
University Library Bulletin, XXI (Winter, 1966),
31-40.

Hummel, Arthur W.   "The Growth of the Orientalia Collections. "   The Library of Congress Quarterly Journal
of Current Acquisitions, XI (February, 1954), 69-87.

Hurewitz, J. C.   Undergraduate Instruction on the Middle
East in American Colleges and Universities.   New
York: American Association for Middle East Studies,
1962.

Inkeles, Alex.   "Understanding a Foreign Society: A Soci-
ologist's View. "   World Politics, III (January, 1951),
269-80.

Jacob, Louis A.   "South Asian Area Studies and the Library: Discussion. "   Library Quarterly, XXXV,
No. 4 (October, 1965), 234-38.

Jelovich, Charles.   "East Central and Southeast European
Studies. "   1967.   (Mimeographed.)

Johnson, Harvey L.   "Latin American Area Programs. "
Hispania, XLIV (May, 1961), 304-07.

Joint Committee on Southern Asia.   "Southern Asia Studies
in the United States; A Survey and Plan. "   [Phila-
delphia, 1951] (Mimeographed.)

Kerr, W. H.   "Acquiring Books on the Far East for a College
Library. "   Far East Quarterly, VI (May, 1947),
300-02.

Kwei, John Chi Ber.   "Bibliographical and Administrative

Problems Arising from the Incorporation of Chinese Books in American Libraries. " Unpublished Ph. D. dissertation, Graduate Library School, University of Chicago, 1931.

Lambert, Richard D. , ed. Resources for South Asian Area Studies in the United States. Philadelphia: University of Pennsylvania Press, 1962.

Legters, Lyman H. "Area Studies and Library Resources: Discussion. " Library Quarterly, XXXV, No. 4 (October, 1965), 217-22.

_____. Language and Area Studies: A Bibliography. New York: New York State Education Department, 1967.

_____. "NDEA Support for Undergraduate Language and Area Studies. " Liberal Education, LI, No. 2 (May, 1965), 278-83.

LeVine, Robert A. "African Studies in American Libraries: Discussion. " Library Quarterly, XXXV, No. 4 (October, 1965), 308-309.

Lindbeck, John M. H. "China: Guidelines for the Implementation of the International Education Act of 1966. " [May, 1967] (Mimeographed.)

McNiff, Philip J. "Foreign Area Studies and Their Effect on Library Development. " College and Research Libraries, XXIV, No. 4 (July, 1963), 291-96, 304-05.

Manning, Clarence A. History of Slavic Studies in the United States. Milwaukee, Wisc. : Marquette University Press, 1957.

Matthew, Robert John. Language and Area Studies in the Armed Services: Their Future Significance. Washington, D. C. : American Council on Education, 1947.

Metter, Paul. "African Studies in the United States: Report for the Department of Health, Education and Welfare. " [1967]. (Mimeographed.)

Mid-European Studies Center. Free Europe Committee. Area Study Programs: The Soviet Union and Eastern

Europe. Urbana, Ill. : University of Illinois, Institute of Government and Public Affairs, 1955.

Miller, Kent, and Fort, Gilberto V. "Staffing of Latin
American Research Collections in the United States. "
Fourteenth Seminar on the Acquisition of Latin American Library Materials, Working Paper No. 8 [Wash-
ington, D. C. : Pan American Union, 1969].

Mintz, Sidney W. A Sample Survey of Area Programs at
American Universities. [New Haven, Conn. : Human
Relations Area File, n. d.].

Morehouse, Ward. "Adding a New Dimension to Liberal
Education. " Liberal Education, XLVI (October, 1960),
380-87.

_____, ed. Asian Studies in Liberal Arts Colleges.
Washington, D. C. : Association of American Colleges,
1961.

_____, ed. Foreign Area Studies and the College Li-
brary. [New York: New York State Education Department, 1965].

_____. The International Dimension of Education in
New York State. [Albany, N. Y. : University of the
State of New York, 1963].

_____. Myopia in the College: A Prescription for
its Relief. Albany, N. Y. : University of the State of
New York, 1964.

_____. "What Should be the Role of Area Programs
in the '60's?" Current Issues in Higher Education,
1960. Washington, D. C. : Association for Higher
Education, 1960.

Morley, James William. "Japan in American Education. "
Prepared for the Department of Health, Education and
Welfare. [May, 1967]. (Mimeographed.)

Morton, Ward M. "The Library and Latin American Studies
Programs. " Fourth Seminar on the Acquisition of
Latin American Library Materials, Final Report and
Papers. [Washington, D. C. : Pan American Union,
1960].

Moses, Larry, comp. Language and Area Study Programs in American Universities. Washington, D. C. : Department of State, External Research Staff, 1964.

Murphy, Franklin D. "Languages and the National Interest." PMLA Bulletin, LXXV (May, 1960), 25-29.

Musgrave, John. "The Southeast Asia Program and the Library: Discussion." Library Quarterly, XXXV, No. 4 (October, 1965), 253-59.

Neuman, Stephanie, and Singman, Sara. "The Southeast Asia Specialist: A Preliminary Report." The American Behavioral Scientist, V (June, 1962), 9-14.

Ng, Tung King. "Librarianship in East Asian Studies." Canadian Library Journal, XXVII, No. 2 (March-April, 1970), 102-14.

Nostrand, Howard Lee. "On Teaching Foreign Culture." Modern Language Journal, XL (October, 1956), 297-301.

_____, et al. Research on Language Teaching: An Annotated International Bibliography for 1945-61. Seattle, Wash. : University of Washington Press, 1962.

Nunn, G. Raymond. "East-West Center Research Collection." Hawaii Library Association Journal, XX (Fall, 1963), 9-11.

_____, and Tsien, Tsuen-Hsuin. "Far Eastern Resources in American Libraries." Library Quarterly, XIX, No. 1 (January, 1959), 27-42.

Panofsky, Hans E. "African Studies in American Libraries." Library Quarterly, XXXV, No. 4 (October, 1965), 298-307.

Parker, William Riley. The National Interest and Foreign Languages. U. S. Department of State Publication No. 7324. 3rd ed. Washington, D. C. : Department of State, 1962.

Parsons, James J. "The Contribution of Geography to Latin American Studies." Social Science Research on Latin

America.   Edited by Charles Wagley.   New York:
Columbia University Press, 1964.

Partington, David H.   "The Islamic Near East: Intellectual
Role of Librarianship: Discussion. "   Library Quarterly, XXXV No. 4 (October, 1965), 294-97.

Patterson, Maureen L. P.   "South Asian Area Studies and
the Library. "   Library Quarterly, XXXV, No. 4
(October, 1965), 223-34.

Poleman, Horace I.   "American Research Library Resources
and Needs for Support of Studies of South Asia. "
Resources for South Asian Area Studies in the United
States.   Edited by Richard D. Lambert.   Philadelphia:
University of Pennsylvania Press, 1962.

Redfield, Robert.   "Area Programs in Education and Research. "   [Washington, D. C. :   Social Science Research
Council, April, 1944].   (Mimeographed.)

Reichmann, Felix.   "Acquisition of Library Materials from
Southeast Asia. "   Library Resources and Technical
Services, VII, No. 1 (Winter, 1963), 13-21.

Rivlin, Benjamin.   "Undergraduate Middle East Courses:
The Area Studies Approach. "   American Association
of Middle East Studies Newsletter, III (Spring, 1962),
1-2, 11.

Ruggles, Melville J.   "Area Studies Embracing the Slavic
World . . . "   [December 1, 1964].   (Mimeographed.)

_____, and Mostecky, Vaclav.   Russian and East
European Publications in Libraries in the United
States.   New York: Columbia University Press, 1960.

Sayres, William C.   The Non-Western World in New York
State Higher Education.   Albany, N. Y. :   University
of the State of New York, 1961.

Singer, Milton, et. al.   "Chicago's Non-Western Civilizations
Program. "   Journal of General Education, XII (January, 1959), 22-49.

_____, ed.   Introducing India in Liberal Education.
Chicago: University of Chicago Press, 1957.

_____ . "The Social Sciences in Non-Western Studies. " Annals of the American Academy of Political and Social Science, CCCLVI (November, 1964), 30-44.

Smith, Wilfred Cantwell. "The Islamic Near East: Intellectual Role of Librarianship. " Library Quarterly, XXXV, No. 4 (October, 1965), 283-94.

_____ . "The Place of Oriental Studies in a Western University. " Diogenes, XVI (Winter, 1956), 104-11.

Social Science Research in Latin America. Seminar on Latin American Studies in the United States, Stanford, California, 1963. New York: Columbia University Press, 1964.

Stevens, Rolland E. "Library Support of Area Study Programs. " College and Research Libraries, XXIV, No. 5 (September, 1963), 383-91.

Steward, Julian H. Area Research, Theory and Practice. Social Science Research Council Bulletin No. 63. New York: Social Science Research Council, 1950.

Stow, Shirley. "Look to the East. " Library Journal, XCI (August, 1966), 3645-46.

Suzuki, Yukihisa. "Role of a Bibliographer in a Japanese Collection. " College and Research Libraries, XXI, No. 3 (May, 1960), 241-46.

Swift, Richard N. World Affairs and the College Curriculum. Washington, D. C. : American Council on Education, 1959.

Taylor, Alan R. African Studies Research. Bloomington, Ind. : Indiana University, African Studies Program, 1964.

Taylor, George E. "The Leadership of the University. " The Non-Western World in Higher Education. Edited by Donald N. Bigelow and Lyman H. Legters. Philadelphia: American Academy of Political and Social Science, 1964.

Tsien, Tsuen-Hsuin, Asian Studies and State Universities; Proceedings of a Conference at Indiana University,

November 11-13, 1959.   Bloomington, Ind. :   Indiana
University, 1960.

_____.   "East Asian Collections in America. "   Li-
brary Quarterly, XXXV, No. 4 (October, 1965),
260-75.

_____.   "First Chinese-American Exchange of Publi-
cations. "   Harvard Journal of Asiatic Studies, XXV
(1964- 65), 19-30.

_____.   "Present Status and Personnel Needs of Far
Eastern Collections in America: A Report for the
Committee on American Library Resources on the Far
East of the Association for Asian Studies. " [Wash-
ington, D. C. :   Library of Congress, Chinese and
Korean Section, September 1, 1964].   (Mimeographed.)

Tsuneishi, Warren M.   "Acquisitions of Library Materials
from China, Japan and Korea. "   Library Resources
and Technical Services, VII, No. 1 (Winter, 1963),
28-33.

_____.   "ALA Institute on Library Collections for
Non-Western Studies. "   LC Information Bulletin, XXV
(July 14, 1966), 408-09.

U. S. Department of Health, Education, and Welfare.   Office
of Education.   Language and Area Centers: Report
on the First Two Years.   Washington, D. C. :   Government Printing Office, 1960.

_____.   Language and Area Centers: Title VI Na-
tional Defense Education Act, 1958-1968.   Washington, D. C. :   Government Printing Office, 1968.

_____.   Language Development Program, Title VI,
NDEA of 1958.   Washington, D. C. :   Government
Printing Office, 1960.

_____.   Report on the National Defense Education Act:
Fiscal Year Ending June 30, 1959.   Washington, D. C. :
Government Printing Office, 1960.

_____.   Report on the National Defense Education Act:
Fiscal Year Ending June 30, 1960.   Washington, D. C. :
Government Printing Office, 1961.

_____. Report on the National Defense Education Act: Fiscal Years 1961 and 1962. Washington, D. C. : Government Printing Office, 1963.

U. S. Department of State. Bureau of Intelligence and Research. Language and Area Study Programs in American Universities. Washington, D. C. : Department of State, 1964.

_____. External Research Division. Language and Area Study Programs in American Universities. Washington, D. C. : The Department, 1962.

_____. Office of Intelligence Research. Area Programs in American Universities. International Information and Culture Series No. 38. Washington, D. C. : The Department, December, 1954.

Vella, Walter F. Summary Report; Conference on Resources for Research on Southeast Asia. Honolulu, Hawaii: University of Hawaii, East-West Center, 1963.

Wagley, Charles. Area Research and Training: A Conference Report on the Study of World Areas. Social Science Research Council Pamphlet No. 6. New York: Social Science Research Council, 1948.

Wagman, Frederick H. "The General Research Library and the Area-Studies Programs. " Library Quarterly, XXXV, No. 4 (October, 1965), 343-55.

Williams, Edwin E. "Experience of Farmington Plan in the Latin American Field. " Final Report and Papers of the Seminar on the Acquisition of Latin American Library Materials, June 14-15, 1956. Gainesville, Fla. : University of Florida Libraries, 1956.

Wilson, Howard, and Wilson, Florence. American Higher Education and World Affairs. Washington, D. C. : American Council on Education, 1963.

Winger, Howard W. Education for Area-Studies Librarianship. " Library Quarterly, XXXV, No. 4 (October, 1965), 361-72.

Other Sources Consulted

Ackerman, Nathan W. "Social Role and Total Personality. "
    American Journal of Orthopsychiatry, XXI (January,
    1951), 1-17.

Alvarez, Robert Smyth. "Qualifications of Heads of Li-
    braries in Cities of Over Ten Thousand Population in
    the Seven North-Central States. " Unpublished Ph. D.
    dissertation, Graduate Library School, University of
    Chicago, 1939.

American Academy of Political and Social Science. Annals,
    CCCLVI (November, 1964).

American Library Association. College and University Li-
    brarians and Librarianship: An Examination of Their
    Present Status and Some Proposals for Their Future
    Development. Chicago: American Library Associa-
    tion, 1946.

American Library Directory, 1968-1969. Comp. by Eleanor
    F. Steiner-Prag. 26th ed. New York: R. R. Bowker
    Co. , 1968.

Ash, Lee, ed. A Biographical Directory of Librarians in
    the United States and Canada. 5th ed. Chicago:
    American Library Association, 1970.

_____. Who's Who in Library Service. 4th ed.
    Hamden, Conn. : Shoe String Press. 1966.

Asheim, Lester, ed. Conference on Library Manpower
    Needs and Utilization. Chicago: American Library
    Association, 1967.

Association of Research Libraries. Minutes of the Sixty-
    Fifth Meeting, January 24, 1965. Washington, D. C. :
    Association of Research Libraries, 1965.

_____. Minutes of the Sixty-Second Meeting, January
    13, 1963. Washington: Association of Research Li-
    braries, 1963.

_____. Minutes of the Seventy-Fourth Meeting,
    June 21, 1969. Washington, D. C. : Association of
    Research Libraries, 1969.

Baumgartel, Howard. "The Concept of Role." The Planning of Change. Edited by Warren G. Bennis, Kenneth D. Benne, and Robert Chin. New York: Holt, Rinehart and Winston, 1964.

Bentley, Joseph C., ed. The Counselor's Role. Boston: Houghton-Mifflin Co., 1968.

Bonner, Hubert. Group Dynamics. New York: Ronald Press, 1959.

Bradley, B. W. "Study of the Characteristics, Qualifications, and Succession Patterns of Heads of Large United States Academic and Public Libraries." Unpublished Master's thesis, Graduate School of Library Science, University of Texas, 1968.

Bryant, Alice L. "Public Librarians: A Study of Professional Personnel in the American Public Library." The Public Library Inquiry. Edited by Robert D. Leigh et. al. Chicago: Chicago University Press, 1950.

Byrd, Cecil K. "Subject Specialists in a University Library." College and Research Libraries, XXVII, No. 3 (May, 1966), 191-93.

Burling, J., Lentz, Edith, and Wilson, R. N. The Give and Take in Hospitals. New York: Putnam, 1956.

Carpenter, Raymond Leonard. "The Public Library Executive: A Study of Status and Role." Unpublished Ph. D. dissertation, University of North Carolina, 1968.

Chicago, University. Graduate Library School. Proceedings of the Thirteenth Annual Conference, May 20-22, 1965. Chicago: University of Chicago Press, 1965.

Danton, J. Periam. Book Selection and Collection; A Comparison of German and American University Libraries. New York: Columbia University Press, 1963.

_____. "Doctoral Study in Librarianship in the United States." College and Research Libraries, XX, No. 6 (November, 1959), 435-50.

_____ . "Subject Specialists in National and University Libraries, with Special Reference to Book Selection. " Libri, XVII, No. 1 (1967), 42-58.

Davidson, Chalmers. "The Status of the Librarian in Southern Liberal Arts Colleges. " Unpublished Master's thesis, Graduate Library School, University of Chicago, 1936.

Douglas, Robert Raymond. "The Personality of the Librarian. " Unpublished Ph. D. dissertation, Graduate Library School, University of Chicago, 1957.

Downs, Robert B. "Preparation of Specialists for University Libraries. " Special Libraries, XXXVII (September, 1946), 209-13.

English, T. H. "Problems of Library Special Collections. " Southeastern Librarian, XIII (Fall. 1963), 131-34.

Farley, Richard Alan. "The American Library Executive: An Inquiry into His Concepts of the Functions of His Office. " Unpublished Ph. D. dissertation, Graduate School of Library Science, University of Illinois, 1967.

Fussler, Herman H. "The Bibliographer Working in a Broad Area of Knowledge. " College and Research Libraries, X, No. 3 (July, 1949), 199-202.

Garrett, Henry E. Statistics in Psychology and Education. 4th ed. New York: Longmans, Green and Co. , 1953.

Getzels, J. W. , and Guba, E. G. "Role, Role Conflict, and Effectiveness: An Empirical Study. " American Sociological Review, XIX, No. 2 (April, 1954), 164-75.

Good, Carter V. Essentials of Educational Research. New York: Appleton-Century-Crofts, Inc. , 1966.

Gould, Julius, and Kolb, William L. , eds. A Dictionary of the Social Sciences. New York: The Free Press, 1964.

Goy, Peter A. , ed. A Biographical Directory of Librarians in the Field of Slavic and East European Studies.

Chicago: American Library Association, 1967.

Gross, Edward. Work and Society. New York: Thomas Y. Crowell, 1958.

_____, et. al. Explorations in Role Analysis. New York: John Wiley and Sons, Inc., 1966.

_____, and Trask, Anne E. Men and Women as Elementary School Principals. Final Report No. 2, Contract No. 853 (SAE-8702), U.S. Office of Education. Cambridge, Mass.: Harvard Graduate School of Education, 1964.

Harlow, Neal. "The Present Is Not What It Was." Library Journal, XLLLIX (June 15, 1964), 2527-32.

Haro, Robert P. "The Bibliographer in the Academic Library." Library Resources and Technical Services, XIII, No. 2 (Spring, 1969), 163-69.

_____. "Book Selection in Academic Libraries." College and Research Libraries, XXVIII, No. 2 (March, 1967), 104-06.

Harvey, John F. The Librarian's Career: A Study of Mobility. ACRL Microcard Series No. 85. Rochester, N.Y.: University of Rochester Press for the Association of College and Research Libraries, 1957.

_____. "Variety in the Experience of Chief Librarians." College and Research Libraries, XIX, No. 2 (March, 1958), 107-10.

Horbinson, Frederick, and Myers, Charles A. "The Logic of Management Development." Management of Human Resources. Edited by Paul Pigors, C.A. Myers, an F.T. Marlin. New York: McGraw-Hill, 1964.

Humphreys, Kenneth. "The Subject Specialist in National ar University Libraries." Libri, XVII, No. 1 (1967), 29-41.

Jacobson, Eugene, Charters, W.W., Jr., and Lieberman, Seymour. "The Use of Role Concept in the Study of Complex Organizations." Journal of Social Issues, VII, No. 3 (1951), 18-27.

Kaser, David. "Dispelling Hunches, Intuitions, and Profes-
    sional Mystique." Wilson Library Bulletin, XLI,
    No. 9 (May, 1967), 923-25.

Knapp, Patricia B. "The College Librarian: Sociology of a
    Professional Specialization." College and Research
    Libraries, XVI, No. 1 (January, 1955), 66-72.

Knapp, Robert H. "Changing Functions of the College Pro-
    fessor." The American College. Edited by Nevitt
    Stanford. New York: Wiley, 1962.

Kornhauser, A. , Dubin, R. , and Ross, A. M. Industrial
    Conflict. New York: McGraw-Hill, 1954.

Kraft, Margit. "An Argument for Selectivity in the Acquisi-
    tion of Materials." Library Quarterly, XXXVI, No. 3
    (July, 1967), 284-95.

Leabo, Dick A. Basic Statistics. 3rd ed. Homewood, Ill. :
    Richard D. Irwin, Inc. , 1968.

Levinson, D. J. "Role, Personality and Social Structure in
    the Organizational Setting." Journal of Abnormal and
    Social Psychology, LVIII (1959), 170-80.

Libraries at Large. Edited by Douglas M. Knight and E.
    Shepley Nourse. New York: R. R. Bowker Co. ,
    1969.

Line, M. B. "Libraries for Expanding Universities." Uni-
    versity Quarterly, XIX (December, 1964), 41-55.

Lockwood, D. P. "Cooperative Acquisitions." College and
    Research Libraries, VIII (April, 1947), 110-12.

McCarthy, Stephen A. Report of a Survey of the Library of
    the University of New Hampshire, January-February,
    1949. [The Library, 1949].

McDiarmid, Edwin W. "The Place of Experience in De-
    veloping College and University Librarians." Library
    Quarterly, XII, No. 3 (July, 1942), 614-21.

Martin, Lowell A. "Personnel in Library Surveys." Li-
    brary Surveys. Edited by Maurice F. Tauber and
    I. R. Stephens. New York: Columbia University

Press, 1967.

Merton, Robert K. , and Kitt, Alice S. "Contributions to
the Theory of Reference Group Behavior. " Continuities in Social Research. Edited by Robert K. Merton
and Paul F. Lazarsfeld. Glencoe, Ill. : The Free
Press, 1950.

Metcalf, Keyes D. "Problems of Acquisition Policy in a
University Library. " Harvard Library Bulletin, IV
(Autumn, 1950), 293-303.

Michigan, University. Survey Research Center. Faculty
Appraisal of a University Library. Ann Arbor, Mich. :
University of Michigan Library, 1961.

Morrison, Perry D. "The Career of the Academic Librarian. " Unpublished DLS dissertation, School of Librarianship, University of California, Berkeley, 1960.

_____. The Career of the Academic Librarian; A
Study of the Social Origins, Educational Attainments,
Vocational Experience, and Personality Characteristics
of a Group of American Academic Librarians. Chicago: American Library Association, 1969.

Mosher, F. C. "Research in Public Administration: Some
Notes and Suggestions. " Public Administration Review, XVI (1956), 169-78.

Nash, William V. "Characteristics of Administrative Heads
of Public Libraries in Various Communications Categories. " Unpublished Ph. D. dissertation, Graduate
School of Library Science, University of Illinois, 1964.

Oppenheim, A. N. Questionnaire Design and Attitude Measurement. New York: Basic Books, Inc. , 1966.

Osipow, S. H. Theories of Career Development. New York:
Appleton-Century-Crofts, 1968.

Plate, Kenneth Harry. "Middle Management in University
Libraries: The Development of a Theoretical Model
for Analysis. " Unpublished Ph. D. dissertation, Graduate School of Library Service, Rutgers - The State
University, 1969.

Pollard, Frances M. "Characteristics of Negro College
    Chief Librarians. " College and Research Libraries,
    XXV, No. 4 (July, 1964), 281-84.

Rand Corporation. A Million Random Digits with 100, 000
    Normal Deviates. New York: The Free Press, 1955.

Reagan, Agnes Lytton. "A Study of Certain Factors in In-
    stitutions of Higher Education which Influence Students
    to Become Librarians. " Unpublished Ph. D. disser-
    tation, Graduate School of Library Science, University
    of Illinois, 1957.

Reichmann, Felix. "Acquisitions Librarian as Bibliograph-
    ers. " College and Research Libraries, X (July,
    1949), 203-07.

_____. "Hercules and Antaeus. " The Status of
    American College and University Libraries. Edited
    by Robert B. Downs. ACRL Monograph No. 22.
    Chicago: American Library Association, 1958.

Reissman, Leonard. "A Study of Role Conceptions in
    Bureaucracy. " Social Forces, XXVII (1949), 305-310.

Ryan, Mary Jane. "Career Development of Librarians. "
    Minnesota Libraries, XXII, No. 6 (Summer, 1968),
    174-78.

Sarbin, Theodore R. "Role Theory. " Handbook of Social
    Psychology. Vol. I. Edited by Gardner Lindzey.
    Reading, Mass. : Addison-Wesley, 1954.

Scherer, Henry Howard. "Faculty-Librarian Relationships
    in Selected Liberal Arts Colleges. " Unpublished
    Ed. D. dissertation, School of Education, University
    of Southern California, 1960.

Schiller, Anita R. Characteristics of Professional Personnel
    in College and University Libraries. Final Report,
    Project No. 5-0919-2-22-1, Contract No. OE-6-10-200,
    U. S. Office of Education. Urbana, Ill. : Library Re-
    search Center, Graduate School of Library Science,
    University of Illinois, May, 1968.

Selltiz, Claire, et. al. , eds. Research Methods in Social
    Relations. Rev. ed. New York: Holt, Rinehart and

Winston, 1959.

Siegel, Sidney. Nonparametric Statistics for the Behavioral
    Sciences. New York: McGraw-Hill Book Co. , Inc. ,
    1956.

Stogdil, Ralph M. Individual Behavior and Group Achieve-
    ment. New York: Oxford University Press, 1959.

Stone, Elizabeth W. Factors Related to the Professional
    Development of Librarians. Metuchen, N. J. : Scare-
    crow Press, 1969.

Stouffer, Samuel A. , et. al. Measurement and Prediction.
    Vol. IV. Princeton, N. J. : Princeton University
    Press, 1950.

Super, Donald E. Scientific Careers and Vocational Develop-
    ment Theory. New York: Bureau of Publications,
    Teachers College, Columbia, 1957.

Swank, Raynard C. "Too Much and too Little. " Library
    Resources and Technical Services, III, No. 1 (Winter,
    1959), 20-31.

Tauber, Maurice F. "Measurement and Evaluation of Re-
    search in Library Technical Services. " Research
    Methods in Librarianship: Measurement and Evalua-
    tion. Edited by Herbert Goldhor. Champaign, Ill. :
    University of Illinois, Graduate School of Library
    Science, 1967.

Trumpeter, Margo. "Non-Librarians in the Academic Li-
    brary. " College and Research Libraries, XXIX,
    No. 6 (November, 1968), 461-65.

Tuttle. Helen Welch. "An Acquisitionist Looks at Mr. Haro's
    Bibliographer. " Library Resources and Technical
    Services, XIII, No. 2 (Spring, 1969), 170-74.

U. S. Department of Labor. Women's Bureau. "Fact Sheet
    on Women in Professional and Technical Positions. "
    Washington, D. C. : Women's Bureau, November,
    1966.

Weber, David C. "The Place of 'Professional Specialists'
    on the University Library Staff. " College and Re-

search Libraries, XXVI, No. 5 (September, 1965), 383-88.

Weidner, Edward M. The World Role of Universities. New York: McGraw-Hill, 1962.

Wight, Edward A. "Research in Organization and Administration." Library Trends, VI (October, 1957), 141-46.

_____. On Research Libraries: Statement and Recommendations of the Committee on Research Libraries of the American Council of Learned Societies. Cambridge, Mass.: MIT Press, 1969.

Wilson, Louis R. "The Objectives of the Graduate Library School in Extending the Frontiers of Librarianship." New Frontiers in Librarianship. Chicago: Graduate Library School, University of Chicago, 1940.

Yamane, Taro. Statistics; An Introductory Analysis. 2nd ed. New York: Harper and Row, 1967.

Zimmerman, L. F. "The Academic and Professional Education of College and University Librarians." Unpublished Master's thesis, Graduate School of Library Science, University of Illinois, 1932.

ARL INSTITUTIONS WITH AREA PROGRAMS (1970)

UNIVERSITY OF ALABAMA
    Latin American Studies
    Russian Area Studies

UNIVERSITY OF ARIZONA
    Latin American Studies*
    Oriental Studies*

BOSTON UNIVERSITY
    African Studies*

UNIVERSITY OF CALIFORNIA
    Latin American Studies*
    Slavic Studies*
    South Asian Studies*
    Southeast Asian Studies*

UNIVERSITY OF CALIFORNIA, LOS ANGELES
    African Studies*
    Latin American Studies*
    Near Eastern Studies*
    Oriental Studies*
    Russian and East European Studies*
    South and South East Asian Studies*

UNIVERSITY OF CHICAGO
    African Studies
    Balkan and Slavic Studies*
    Far Eastern Studies*
    Latin American Studies
    Middle East Studies*
    Southern Asian Studies*

COLUMBIA UNIVERSITY
    African Studies Institute*
    East Central Europe Institute*
    East Asian Institute*

        Latin American Studies Institute*
        Middle East Institute*
        Russian Institute*
        Southern Asian Institute*

CORNELL UNIVERSITY
        African Studies
        China Program*
        Latin American Studies*
        Near Eastern Studies
        South Asia Program
        Southeast Asia Studies*
        Soviet Studies*

DUKE UNIVERSITY
        Russia and East Europe Comparative Studies
        Southern Asia Comparative Studies*

UNIVERSITY OF FLORIDA
        Latin American Studies*

FLORIDA STATE UNIVERSITY
        East Asian Studies
        Slavic and East European Studies

GEORGETOWN UNIVERSITY
        Latin American Studies
        Russian Studies

HARVARD UNIVERSITY
        East Asian Studies
        Far Eastern Studies*
        Middle Eastern Studies*
        Russian Center*

JOHNS HOPKINS UNIVERSITY
        Near Eastern Studies

UNIVERSITY OF ILLINOIS
        Asian Studies*
        Latin American Studies*
        Russian Studies*

INDIANA UNIVERSITY
        African Studies*
        East Asian Studies*
        Latin American Studies*

Near Eastern Studies*
Russian and East European Institute*

UNIVERSITY OF KANSAS
    East Asian Studies*
    Latin American Area Studies*
    Slavic and Soviet Area Studies*

UNIVERSITY OF MASSACHUSETTS
    Asian Studies
    Latin American Studies*

UNIVERSITY OF MICHIGAN
    Chinese Studies Center*
    Japanese Studies Center*
    Near East and North African Studies Center*
    Russian Studies Center*
    South and Southeast Asia Studies Center*

MICHIGAN STATE UNIVERSITY
    African Studies Center*
    East Asian Studies*
    Latin American Studies*
    South Asian Studies*

UNIVERSITY OF MINNESOTA
    East and South Asia Area Studies*
    Latin American Area Studies
    Middle East Area Studies*
    Russian Area Studies

NEW YORK UNIVERSITY
    Russian Area Studies*

NORTHWESTERN UNIVERSITY
    African Studies*
    Slavic Studies*

UNIVERSITY OF NOTRE DAME
    African Studies
    Latin American Studies
    Soviet and East European Studies*

OHIO STATE UNIVERSITY
    Far East Studies*
    Latin American Studies*
    Middle East Studies*
    Russian Area Studies*

UNIVERSITY OF OREGON
    Asian Studies
    Latin American Studies

UNIVERSITY OF PENNSYLVANIA
    Oriental Studies*
    Slavic and Baltic Studies
    South Asia Regional Studies*

PENNSYLVANIA STATE UNIVERSITY
    Slavic and Soviet Area Center*

UNIVERSITY OF PITTSBURGH
    Asian Studies*
    Latin American Studies*
    Russian and East European Studies*

PRINCETON UNIVERSITY
    African Studies
    East Asian Studies*
    Latin American Studies*
    Near Eastern Studies*
    Russian Studies*

RUTGERS UNIVERSITY
    Latin American Studies

UNIVERSITY OF SOUTHERN CALIFORNIA
    Asian Studies
    Latin American Studies

SOUTHERN ILLINOIS UNIVERSITY
    Asian Studies
    Inter-American Studies

STANFORD UNIVERSITY
    African Studies*
    East Asian Studies*
    East European Studies*
    Latin American Studies*

SYRACUSE UNIVERSITY
    Asian Studies*
    Latin American Studies*
    Russian Studies*

UNIVERSITY OF TEXAS
    Asian Studies*
    Latin American Studies*
    Middle East Studies*

TEXAS A&M UNIVERSITY
    Latin American Studies

UNIVERSITY OF TORONTO
    East Asian Studies*
    Indian Studies*
    Islamic Studies*
    Latin American Studies*
    Near Eastern Studies*
    Russian and Slavic Studies*

TULANE UNIVERSITY
    Latin American Studies*

UNIVERSITY OF UTAH
    Middle East Center*

UNIVERSITY OF VIRGINIA
    Asian Studies*
    Russian and Communist Studies Center*

WASHINGTON STATE UNIVERSITY
    East European Studies*
    Latin American Studies*

WASHINGTON UNIVERSITY
    Asian Studies*
    Latin American Studies*
    Slavic Studies*

WAYNE STATE UNIVERSITY
    East European Studies

UNIVERSITY OF WISCONSIN
    African Studies*
    East Asian Studies*
    Ibero-American Studies*
    Indian Studies*
    Russian Area Studies*

YALE UNIVERSITY
    African Studies*

East Asian Studies*
Latin American Studies*
Russian and East European Studies*
Southeast Asia Studies*

*Indicates programs served by area specialist bibliographers.
(These listings include only programs which offer advanced
degrees of some sort.   Strictly language programs and all
undergraduate programs are excluded.)

150